Hello and welcome!

Nachdem du neue Wörter in der Schule besprochen hast, kannst du die **New words** in diesem Buch als Vokabelheft benutzen.

Hello and welcome! Ich bin der Wordmaster und helfe dir beim Wörterlernen.

Die **fett gedruckten** deutschen Wörter sind Lernwörter. Sie fehlen im englischen Satz, damit du sie eintragen kannst.

Meine Tipps

1 Die Reihenfolge der **New words** entspricht der Reihenfolge der neuen Wörter im Vocabulary deines Schülerbuches. Dort kannst du deine Lösungen überprüfen.

2 Wenn du mal nicht weiter weißt, kannst du auch im Vocabulary nachschauen.

3 Lern neue Wörter in einem Satz. So kann man sie sich besser merken.

4 Üb den neuen Wortschatz. Deck zum Beispiel mit einem Blatt Papier die englischen Sätze ab und versuch, die deutschen Sätze ins Englische zu übersetzen. Oder umgekehrt.

New words ▸ p. 1

Mein **Name** ist … — My _name_ is …
Ich komme aus Deutschland. — _I'm from_ Germany.
Ich gehe zur **Schule**. — I go to _school_.
Ich **lerne** Englisch. — I _____ English.
Unser **Lehrer** ist nett. — Our _____ is nice.

… das große R bedeutet Revision: Auf Deutsch Wiederholung. Hier übst du Vokabeln, die du bereits früher gelernt hast.

Hi! Ich bin Ken und gebe dir Tipps. Zum Beispiel …

Überhaupt: Es gibt neben **New words** viele lustige Übungen. Die Lösungen findest du im beigelegten Heftchen.

Introduction

New words ▶ pp. 6–7

Hast du schon die **Einführung** gelesen?	Have you read the _____ yet?
Meine **Jugend**gruppe war auf dem **Fest**.	My _____ group was at the _____.
Dieser Fußballstar ist ein **nationaler** Held.	This football star is a _____ hero.
Ist Wales ein Teil des **Vereinten Königreiches**?	Is Wales part of the _____?
Wir trafen Menschen **aus der ganzen Welt**.	We met people _____.
Diese **Art von** Musik ist **genial**.	This _____ music is _____.
Magst du wirklich **klassische** Musik?	Do you really like _____ music?
Ja, und ich gehe oft zu **Konzerten**.	Yes, and I often go to _____.
Lass uns am **Workshop teilnehmen**.	Let's _____ in the _____.
Legt Rob jedes Wochenende **Platten auf**?	Does Rob _____ every weekend?
Aus welchem Land kommt das **Steeldrum**?	What country is the _____ from?
Man braucht **Stahl** um Brücken zu bauen.	You need _____ to build bridges.
Ich kann **Schlagzeug** und **Fiedel** spielen.	I can play the _____ and the _____.
Übrigens habe ich mir eine Gitarre gekauft.	_____, I've bought a guitar.
Im **Norden** ist es meistens kälter.	It's usually colder in the _____

1 Lost words

Ergänze die Sätze mit den Wörtern im Feuerwerk.

1 _____ his youth grandpa was a very good swimmer.

2 What kind _____ music do your parents like?

3 People _____ all over Germany came to the concert.

4 What's the shortest way _____ the hostel?

5 There were three different bands _____ the gig.

6 _____ the way, where did you buy the steel drum?

7 B comes _____ C in the alphabet.

8 And D comes _____ C and E.

between, of, before, to, by, in, from, at

Introduction

New words ▶ pp. 8–9

Wir verbrachten die Woche in einer **Herberge**.	We spent the week in a _____.
Kannst du ein **Instrument** spielen?	Can you play an _____?
Wer ist der **Chef** hier?	Who's the _____ here?
Unsere Band hat jeden Monat einen **Auftritt**.	Our band does a _____ every month.
eine **Mischung** aus Jazz und klassischer Musik	a _____ of jazz and classical music
Wir spielen nicht nur **westliche** Musik.	We don't just play _____ music.

2 Verb forms

Ergänze die Tabelle der unregelmäßigen Verben.

1	keep	kept	kept
2		showed	
3	spend		
4	hide		
5		did	
6			taken

7	fly		
8		read	
9			thrown
10			spoken
11		wrote	
12	ride		

3 Crossword

Die Buchstabenrätsel helfen dir, die Lösungen zu finden. (↓ →)

2 across: P R A C T I S E

Across →
2 How long do you ★ the piano every day? (8)
4 TAURIG: You can find an instrument in these letters. (6)
5 In a ★, people sing and/or play music. (4)
7 – What can I do at the festival today?
   – Look at the ★ It has all the information. (9)
8 a famous singer, actor, etc. (4)
11 Nice to listen to: people sing it or play it on instruments (5)
12 I like this band best. It's my ★ band. (9)

Down ↓
1 MURD: You can find an instrument in these letters. (4)
2 This instrument has a black and white keyboard. (5)
3 Sue loves singing. She'd like to be a ★ in a band. (6)
6 great, super, very good (9)
7 What instrument do you ★?(4)
8 You sing it. (4)
9 Maybe one day I'll be rich and ★. (6)
10 You need one to get into the theatre or cinema. (6)

4 Introduction

New words ▶ pp. 10–11

Warst du jemals in den **Vereinigten Staaten**?	Have you been to the _____?
Wie wär's mit einer Pizza?	_____ a pizza?
Nein danke, ich bin nicht **hungrig**.	No, thanks. I'm not _____.
Nett, dich kennenzulernen.	_____
Eine halbe Stunde später kam er.	He came _____ later.
Er gab mir die **Hälfte** seiner Brote.	He gave me _____ of his sandwiches.
Lass uns **in Verbindung bleiben**.	Let's _____.
Wird Tim auf der Party sein? – **Wart's ab!**	Will Tim be at the party? – _____!
eine neue **Aufnahme** eines alten Lieds	a new _____ of an old song
Welches Bild **passt zu** welchem Wort?	Which picture _____ which word?
Kannst du **elektrische** Gitarre spielen?	Can you play the _____ guitar?
Willst du **Querflöte** lernen?	Do you want to learn the _____?
Nein. Ich möchte **Blockflöte** lernen.	No. I'd like to learn the _____.
Wann hat er angefangen **Saxophon** zu spielen?	When did he start to play the _____?
Kann jemand hier **Trompete** spielen?	Can anyone here play the _____?
Und wer spielt **Geige**?	And who plays the _____?

4 Last letter – first letter

Der letzte Buchstabe von jedem Wort ist gleichzeitig der erste des nächsten Wortes.

1 Trommel
2 Mischung
3 elektrisch
4 Konzert
5 Trompete
6 Posaune
7 genug
8 Hälfte
9 Fiedel
10 Aufzug (AE)
11 Blockflöte

5 Word search

Finde im Gitter 9 Musikinstrumente.
Schreibe dann das englische Wort mit der deutschen Übersetzung auf. (↓ →)

M	V	I	O	L	I	N	V	R	W
S	G	X	P	I	A	N	O	R	M
R	U	X	Q	K	T	H	V	E	F
B	I	D	L	X	J	V	S	C	L
F	T	R	U	M	P	E	T	O	U
I	A	F	J	O	P	Q	H	R	T
D	R	L	I	D	R	U	M	D	E
D	Q	X	Y	A	H	C	F	E	T
L	Q	S	Q	A	L	O	M	R	N
E	S	A	X	O	P	H	O	N	E

violin – Geige

6 Word groups

Trage die Wörter von der Wiese in die richtigen Kletterseile ein.

clothes

jobs

places in town

animals

engineer dress deer department store fireman frog hedgehog hospital
hostel jacket leisure centre mole paramedic police station policewoman pyjamas
restaurant shoes skirt squirrel teacher trousers waiter woodpecker

Unit 1

New words ▶ p. 12

London ist die **Hauptstadt** von Großbritannien.	London is the _____ of Great Britain.
Die Aussicht vom **Riesenrad** ist toll.	The view from the _____ is fantastic.
Schau, dieses Auto hat nur drei **Räder**.	Look. This car has only got three _____ .
Hohe Gebäude haben meistens einen Fahrstuhl.	_____ buildings usually have a lift.
Wie heißt das deutsche **Parlament**?	What's the name of the German _____ ?
eine **Tondatei** kopieren	copy a _____
einen **schicken** Rock kaufen	buy a _____ skirt
Kleider **aus zweiter Hand** sind oft billig.	_____ clothes are often cheap.

1 Word friends

In jedem Haus gibt es drei Wörter bzw. Wortverbindungen, die man direkt nach dem Verb auf der Fahne benutzen kann. Unterstreiche sie.

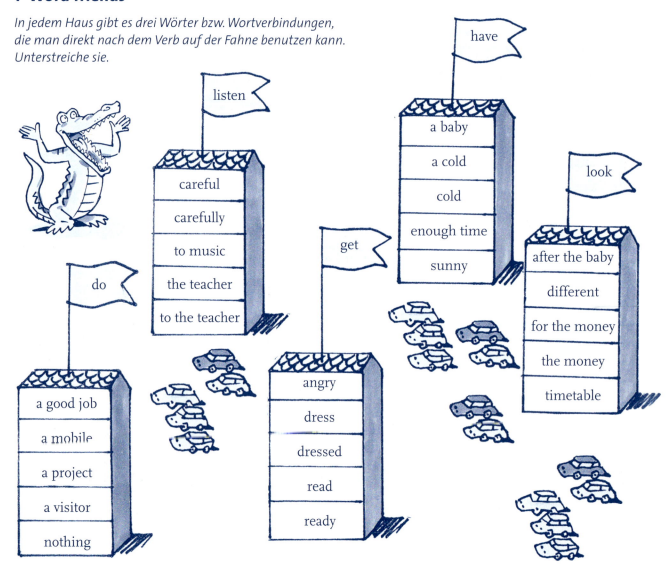

1

New words ▶ p. 13

Er öffnete das **Tor** und verließ den Garten.	He opened the _____ and left the garden.
Lebt die **königliche** Familie in diesem Schloss?	Does the _____ family live in this castle?
Manchmal kann man die **Königin** sehen.	Sometimes you can see the _____ .
Im Sommer gibt es Konzerte **im Freien**.	In summer there are _____ concerts.
Sie warf den Ball hoch in die **Luft**.	She threw the ball high in the _____ .
Die **Haupt**einkaufsstraße hat viele Läden.	The _____ shopping street has lots of shops.
Ich **horchte aufs** Telefon, aber es klingelte nicht.	I _____ the phone, but it didn't ring.
Wie **heißt** die Hauptstadt von Wales?	What _____ the capital of Wales _____ ?
Kannst du das Lied für mich **aufnehmen**?	Can you _____ this song for me?
einen **Tagesausflug** aufs Land machen	have a _____ in the country
Ich habe **überall** nach dem Schlüssel geschaut.	I've looked _____ for the key.

2 Word ladder

Gehe von unten nach oben, indem du bei jeder Sprosse einen Buchstaben veränderst.

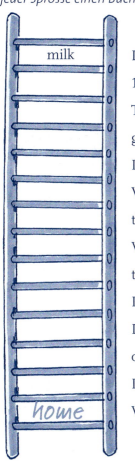

Do you take ★ in your tea?

1.6 km = 1 ★.

This pen isn't ★. Is it yours?

good, OK

I don't understand this word in the first ★ of the text.

We live in the little house at the end of this ★.

the opposite of 'early'

What ★ is your birthday? – February 5th.

the opposite of 'love'

I'm staying in bed today because I ★ a cold.

Don't spend all your pocket money. Try and ★ some.

opposite of 'different'

I need ★ stamps for these postcards.

We didn't go out yesterday – we stayed at ★.

8 **1**

New words ▸ pp. 14–15

In London fahre ich immer mit der **U-Bahn**.　In London I always travel by _____ .

Hat jeder Bahnhof einen **Fahrkartenschalter**?　Does every station have a _____ ?

Drei **einfache Fahrkarten** kosten mehr　Three _____ cost more

... als eine **Tagesfahrkarte**.　... than a _____ .

Es gibt viel Verkehr in der **Hauptverkehrszeit**.　There's lots of traffic in the _____ .

Erwachsene müssen mehr als Kinder zahlen.　_____ have to pay more than children.

die beste **Art und Weise**, eine Sprache zu lernen　the best _____ to learn a language

Fahren alle **Linien** in die Stadtmitte?　Do all _____ go to the city centre?

die Hauptstädte von **Mittel**europa besuchen　visit the capitals of Europe

Nimm die District Line in **Richtung Osten**.　Take the District Line _____ .

Ihr müsst am nächsten Bahnhof **umsteigen**.　You have to _____ at the next station.

Unser Zug fährt vom **Bahnsteig** 2.　Our train goes from _____ 2.

Früher einmal war hier eine Brücke.　_____ there was a bridge here.

Wo kann man heute **über** den Fluss gehen?　Where can you go _____ the river today?

3 Definitions

*Vervollständige die Definitionen mit Wörtern
aus den Mauersteinen. Trage die richtigen Wörter
aus Kens Zeitung in die rechte Spalte ein.*

wheels　concert
hostel　capital
sights　queen

	important	hotel	country	four	photos		
	spend	lots	king	move	places	live	woman

1　A car needs them to *move* and usually has _____ of them.　*wheels*

2　the most _____ city in a _____　_____

3　interesting _____ in a city. tourists often take _____ of them　_____

4　an important _____ , often the wife of a _____　_____

5　a place to _____ the night, usually cheaper than a _____　_____

6　_____ music for _____ of people　_____

4 More about ... London Underground

Vervollständige den Text mit den Wörtern aus der Box.

~~also~~ although and because before but more only too when

London Underground

London Underground is the oldest underground railway in the world. People _also_ (1) call it the 'Tube' _____ (2) the tunnels look like *tubes. The first line opened in 1863. It was _____ (3) six kilometres long. The first electric trains came in 1890; _____ (4) that, there were *steam trains. Today there are 12 lines _____ (5) 275 stations. Together all the lines are 408 kilometres long, _____ (6) only 185 kilometres are under the ground. Outside the city centre, the lines run over ground _____ (7). In 1863, _____ (8) the Underground opened, 41,000 people travelled on the first day. Today _____ (9) than 3 million people use the Tube every day. _____ (10) it's more expensive than the bus and you don't see as much of London, it's the fastest way to travel around the city.

tube = Röhre; steam train = Dampfzug

5 Crossword: places in a city

Die Buchstabenrätsel helfen dir, die Lösungen zu finden. (↓ →)

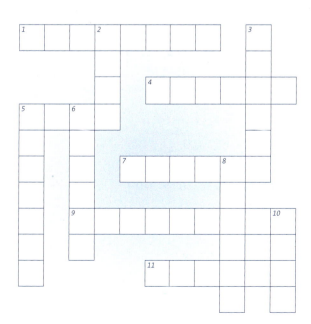

Across
1 ISOPHTAL: You can get help here if you're ill. (8)
4 EUUMMS: Go to this place to see old and interesting things. (6)
5 KCLO: a kind of lift for boats (4)
7 CAPELA: Kings and queens live here. (6)
9 DALERCATH: a very important church (9)
11 MOLCUN There's a statue of Nelson on top of one. (6)

Down
2 KRAP: Go here to walk, relax or play. (4)
3 SERQUA: a place with buildings on four sides (6)
5 RIBALRY: You can find lots of books here. (7)
6 RUCHCH: a building, often with a tower – some people go there on Sundays (6)
8 SICCUR: a round place with buildings around it (6)
10 NALE: a kind of road (4)

New words ▶ pp. 16–17

Ein Geschenk! Das eine schöne **Überraschung**.	A present! That's a nice _____.
Er war **überrrascht**, als ich plötzlich hineinkam.	He was _____ when I suddenly came in.
Ist er Engländer? – Nein. **Eigentlich** ist er Waliser.	Is he English? – No. _____ he's Welsh.
Das große Gebäude da drüben ist eine **Moschee**.	The big building over there is a _____.
Ich hasse RnB! **Aber egal**, die CD ist zu teuer.	I hate RnB! _____, the CD is too expensive.
Möchtest du ein **Currygericht** oder eine Pizza?	Would you like _____ or a pizza?
Magst du lieber **würzige** oder **milde** Gerichte?	Do you like _____ or _____ dishes better?
Die Suppe riecht **seltsam**. Ist sie in Ordnung?	The soup smells _____. Is it OK?
Igitt! Dieser Tee ist viel zu stark.	_____! This tea is much too strong.

6 Hidden words

Ergänze die Wortgruppen, indem du Wörter mit Buchstaben des Wortes „parliament" bildest.

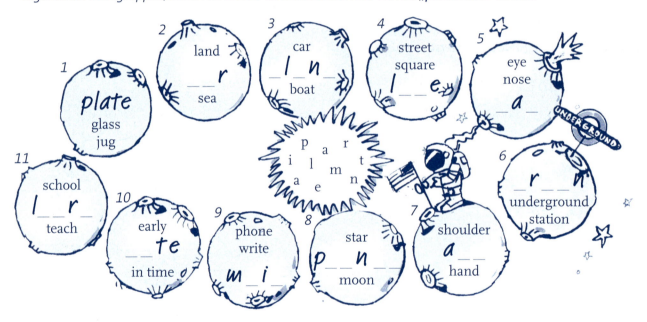

7 Word families

Finde die passenden Verben zu den angegebenen Nomen.

1 explanation – *explain*   5 actor – _____   9 rehearsal – _____

2 winner – _____   6 laughter – _____   10 glue – _____

3 smile – _____   7 building – _____   11 movement – _____

4 flight – _____   8 description – _____   12 explorer – _____

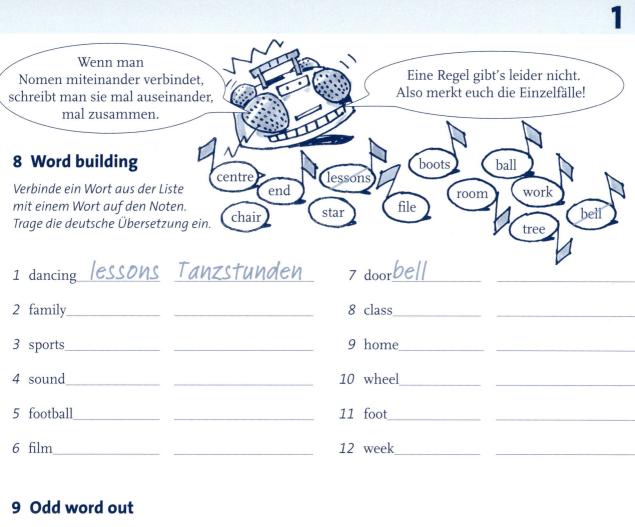

8 Word building

Verbinde ein Wort aus der Liste mit einem Wort auf den Noten. Trage die deutsche Übersetzung ein.

1 dancing _lessons_ _Tanzstunden_
2 family_____ _____
3 sports_____ _____
4 sound_____ _____
5 football_____ _____
6 film_____ _____
7 door_bell_ _____
8 class_____ _____
9 home_____ _____
10 wheel_____ _____
11 foot_____ _____
12 week_____ _____

9 Odd word out

Ein Wort passt nicht. Finde und unterstreiche es.

1 mosque – palace – museum – adult
2 giraffe – budgie – hippo – rhino
3 recorder – CD player – trumpet – flute
4 trendy – sweet – mild – spicy
5 potato – carrot – dish – banana
6 planet – sun – ball – moon

10 The best word

Finde das Wort in der Strickleiter, das am besten in die Lücke passt.

1 Why are you so _____ with me? I haven't done anything wrong.

2 Paul is so _____ . He even finds it hard to say hello to people.

3 Kim felt very _____ when she won the first prize.

4 Rob looked _____ . He didn't understand the joke.

5 Don't be _____ . The dog really isn't dangerous.

6 We were a bit _____ before the test, but it was actually OK.

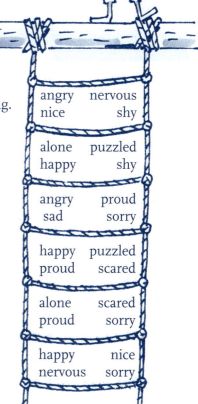

New words ▶ pp. 20–25

die **Beförderung** zwischen Bahnhof und Hotel	_____ between station and hotel
ein Tunnel unter dem **Erdboden**	a tunnel under the _____
Mit dieser **Maschine** kannst du Brot machen.	You can make bread with this _____.
Ich will einen Englisch**kurs** in England machen.	I want do to an English _____ in England.
Diese **Bäckerei** macht das beste Brot.	This _____ makes the best bread.
Unser **Fleischer** macht die besten Würstchen.	Our _____ makes the best sausages.
Papa mag viel **Butter** auf dem Brot.	Dad likes lots of _____ on his bread.
Wir brauchen Obst und **Gemüse**.	We need fruit and _____.
Wir sind bloß eine normale **Alltags**familie.	We're just a normal _____ family.
War diese **Durchsage** für unseren Zug?	Was that _____ for our train?
Warum hast du deine **Reise unterbrochen**?	Why did you _____ your _____ ?

11 Word search

Finde im Rätsel 15 deutsche Begriffe zum Thema Verkehr. Schreibe dann das deutsche Wort und die englische Übersetzung auf. (↓ →)

S	T	R	A	S	S	E	N	B	A	H	N
U	D	B	A	H	N	H	O	F	M	U	M
E	I	N	S	T	E	I	G	E	N	M	Q
F	L	U	G	H	A	F	E	N	C	S	A
L	M	X	J	D	Z	W	G	H	I	T	U
U	Q	F	L	U	G	Z	E	U	G	E	T
G	Q	T	A	X	I	J	Q	H	F	I	O
S	F	A	H	R	P	L	A	N	A	G	P
T	Z	A	U	S	S	T	E	I	G	E	N
E	Z	T	B	U	S	W	U	E	U	N	E
I	U	F	M	S	F	A	E	H	R	E	K
G	G	B	A	H	N	S	T	E	I	G	T

Straßenbahn – tram
_____
_____
_____
_____
_____
_____
_____
_____
_____
_____
_____
_____
_____
_____

New words ▸ pp. 26–27

Wie **funktioniert** diese Maschine?

How does this machine _____ ?

Es ist sicherer, einen Fahrrad**helm** zu tragen.

It's safer to wear a bike _____ .

Was steht auf dem **Schild**?

What does the _____ say?

Ruf die Polizei, wenn du in **Gefahr** bist.

Call the police if you're in _____ .

Brände können Gebäude **zerstören**.

Fires can _____ buildings.

Das Abendessen ist **beinahe** fertig.

Dinner is _____ ready.

Drück auf den **Knopf** und die Tür wird aufgehen.

Push the _____ and the door will open.

Vor einem Flug bin ich immer **aufgeregt**.

I'm always _____ before a flight.

Kannst du bitte einen **Moment** warten?

Can you wait a _____ , please?

nahe am Meer, und nicht weit von London

_____ the sea, and not far from London

Wo **Rauch** ist, ist auch Feuer.

Where there's _____ there's fire.

Es is nicht gesund, Tabak zu **rauchen**.

It isn't healthy to _____ tobacco.

Nach dem Regen waren die Straßen **nass**.

After the rain the roads were _____ .

Dieser Plan ist nicht sehr **realistisch**.

This plan isn't very _____ .

Er ist **freundlich** und lächelt immer.

He's _____ and always smiles.

Ich war in großer Gefahr und **schrie** um Hilfe.

I was in great danger and _____ for help.

Zieh bitte den **Stecker** nicht heraus.

Please don't pull out the _____ .

Ohne **Strom** funktioniert kein Computer.

No computer works without _____ .

12 Opposites

Trage die Gegenteile der fett gedruckten Wörter in die Lücken ein.

1 an **international** / a _national_ festival

2 Do you like **mild** / _____ dishes?

3 This room is very **dirty** / _____ .

4 Turn **left** / _____ at the next corner.

5 whisper **quietly** / shout _____

6 a **strong** / _____ person

7 It's **possible** / _____ to get there by bus.

8 Are you planning to **arrive** / _____ early?

9 Only **poor** / _____ people live in this street.

10 Is the supermarket **open** / _____ ?

11 buy a **return** / _____ ticket

12 She has lots of **enemies** / _____ .

New words ▸ pp. 28–29

ein **Lichtblitz** am Himmel — a _____ in the sky

Ich kenne das Wort nicht. Was **bedeutet** es? — I don't know the word. What does it _____?

Die Geschichte hatte kein glückliches **Ende**. — The story didn't have a happy _____.

meiner Meinung nach ... — _____ ...

Wie komme ich voran? — _____?

Wir wohnen in einer ruhigen **Gegend**. — We live in a quiet _____.

Fakten und Daten sind in Geschichte wichtig — _____ and dates are important in history.

13 Pronunciation

Ordne die Wörter aus der Box der richtigen Aussprachegruppe zu.

Wenn ihr mal Probleme mit der Aussprache habt, hilft die Lautschrift im Dictionary!

already beach bread breakfast cheap clean
clear dead dear disappear ear eastbound
head idea leave meant near tea

e	iː	ɪə
already	clean	dear
_____	_____	_____
_____	_____	_____
_____	_____	_____
_____	_____	_____
_____	_____	_____

14 One or two letters?

Trage die fehlenden Buchstaben ein:
d *oder* **dd**, **f** *oder* **ff**, **n** *oder* **nn**.

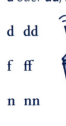

d dd   fi____le, mi____le, stu____ent, hi____en, rea____y, mo____el

f ff   a____raid, gira____e, tra____ic, o____ten, di____icult, le____t

n nn   a____other, begi____ing, di____er, tu____el, e____emy, pe____cil

15 Hour glasses

Übersetze die Wörter und trage sie in die passende Sanduhr ein.

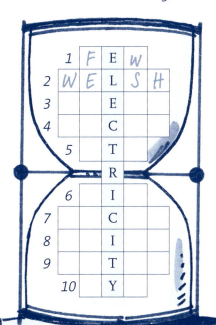
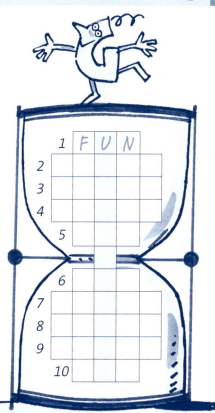

1 ein paar/einige – Spaß
2 Geld – walisisch
3 heute – sauber
4 Feind – Tatsachen
5 aß – Arm
6 Mülltonne – Kunst
7 Rauch – Schinkenspeck
8 Rock – Flöte
9 nachdem – sonnig
10 hinzufügen – Auge

Die geheime Wort in der rechten Sanduhr heißt: Englisch _____

Deutsch _____

16 Picture puzzle

Vergleiche die beiden Bilder miteinander. Welche 8 Gegenstände fehlen auf dem rechten Bild?

a purse _____   _____

_____   _____

_____   _____

Unit 2

New words ▸ p. 30

Ein **Lachs** ist ein großer Fisch. — A _____ is a large fish.

hoch auf der **Klippe** über dem Meer — high on the _____ above the sea

Um die Insel herum liegen viele **Felsen**. — There are lots of _____ around the island.

Wir brauchen etwas **Öl** für unseren Salat. — We need some _____ for our salad.

Der **Bauer** verkaufte sein Gemüse auf dem Markt. — The _____ sold his vegetables at the market.

1 Word friends

Welche Wörter aus den Kieselsteinen passen in die Lücken?

1 _eat_ salmon / a big meal / too much

2 _____ for a bus / for 10 minutes / outside

3 _____ a ball / a thief / the bank robbers

4 _____ a good book / and write / a brochure

5 _____ two languages / more slowly / to me

6 _____ to the radio / for the doorbell

7 _____ all the answers / lots of people

8 _____ crosswords / your homework / judo

9 _____ a teacher / tired / very excited

10 _____ in touch / the window open

2 The fourth word

Welches Wort fehlt hier?

1 apple – fruit   onion – _____

2 good – bad   clever – _____

3 meat – butcher's   bread – _____

4 build – building   fly – _____

5 cow – beef   pig – _____

6 up – down   top – _____

7 ridden – ride   forgotten – _____

8 heard – hear   taught – _____

9 husband – husbands   wife – _____

3 Odd word out

Unterstreiche das Wort, das nicht passt.

1 car – farm – bus – bike

2 mountain – lake – farmer – cliff

3 danger – farmer – butcher – waiter

4 onion – mushroom – salmon – pea

5 lorry – ferry – boat – ship

6 tired – hungry – cold – station

7 first – second – three – fourth

8 first – west – north – south

9 mail – write – wait – phone

New words ▶ p. 32

Wie lange **dauert** der Flug nach Berlin?	How long does the flight to Berlin _____ ?
Ohne Brille **konnte** er nicht lesen.	He wasn't _____ to read without glasses.
Ich kann dich am Flughafen **abholen**.	I can _____ you _____ at the airport.
Die **Ankunfts**zeit ist jeden Tag dieselbe.	The _____ time is the same every day.
Wann werden wir **ankommen**?	When will we _____ ?
Kannst du mir die **Abfahrts**zeit sagen?	Can you tell me the _____ time?
Er kam früh und blieb **bis** 13 Uhr.	He came early and stayed _____ 1 pm.
Der Laden ist geöffnet **von** Montag **bis** Sonnabend.	The shop opens _____ Monday _____ Saturday.

4 Scrambled words: school

Löse die Buchstabenrätsel, um Wörter zu finden, die mit Schule zusammenhängen.
Trage die deutschen Übersetzungen ein. Die markierten Buchstaben ergeben das „geheime Wort".

1 Teal Bit Em — T I M E T A B L E — Stundenplan
2 Trace Eh — _____ _____
3 Cam Tassel — _____ _____
4 Hay Idols — _____ _____
5 Bad Or — _____ _____
6 Sic Enec — _____ _____
7 Carom Loss — _____ _____

5 Word groups

Übersetze die deutschen Wörter auf den Zetteln ins Englische und füge sie in die richtige Wortgruppe ein.

farm animals	media	transport
chicken		

Handy, Schaf, Lamm, Zeitung, Abfahrt, Bahnhof, Truthahn, Huhn, Kuh, Pferd, Radio, Zeitschrift, Fernsehen, Ankunft, U-Bahn, Fahrplan, Bushaltestelle, Tondatei

New words ▶ p. 33

Meine Eltern mögen keine **elektronische** Musik.	My parents don't like _____ music.
die neuen **Medien** wie das Internet oder E-Mail	the new _____ like the internet or e-mail
Er hatte keine Freunde und fühlte sich **einsam**.	He had no friends and felt _____ .
Mein **Urgroßvater** wird dieses Jahr 90 Jahre alt.	My _____ will be 90 this year.
Ich hatte nicht viel **Post** – nur einen Brief.	I didn't have much _____ – only one letter.
Ich sah ihn nur **einmal**.	I only saw him _____ .
Oder war es **zweimal**?	Or was it _____ ?
Der Arzt kommt drei Mal **pro** Woche.	The doctor comes three times _____ week.
Stell dir vor, du bist eine Katze.	_____ you're a cat.
Schick mir bitte eine **SMS**.	Please send me a _____ .
Ich habe eine wichtige **Nachricht** für dich.	I've got important _____ for you.
Kannst du mir die Nummer **per SMS schicken**?	Can you _____ me the number?
Rob und ich sind immer gute **Kumpel** gewesen.	Rob and I have always been good _____ .
Es ist **persönlich**. Ich möchte nicht darüber reden.	It's _____ . I don't want to talk about it.
Ich habe einen neuen **Klingelton** für mein Handy.	I've got a new _____ for my mobile.
den ganzen Abend **im Internet surfen**	_____ all evening
Wir können diese zwei Lieder **mischen**.	We can _____ these two songs.

6 Last letter – first letter

Der letzte Buchstabe von jedem Wort ist gleichzeitig der erste des nächsten Wortes.

1 Fahrplan
2 aufgeregt
3 Abfahrt
4 Elefant
5 dauern/(Zeit) brauchen
6 Aufzug
7 Fels
8 Schlüssel
9 du/ihr/dir/euch
10 bis
11 einsam
12 gähnen

2   19

7 Spot the mistakes

In jedem Satz sind zwei Fehler. Unterstreiche und korrigiere sie. Es gibt Rechtschreib- und grammatische Fehler.

1 Hoy is one of the biger Orkney ilands.   *bigger*   _____

2 Live on an island can be lonly sometimes.   _____   _____

3 Katrina have a mobil, so she often texts her friends.   _____   _____

4 She also write e-mails once or twice a weak.   _____   _____

5 She sometimes downloads musik from a webseite.   _____   _____

8 Making phrases

Vervollständige die Audrücke mit dem Verb vom richtigen Zettel.

1 *take* _____ a photo of the cows in the field

2 _____ a text message to a friend

3 _____ the arrival times in the timetable

4 _____ all the hungry farm animals

5 _____ the train at the next station

6 _____ your mum on your mobile

take · check · get off · phone · send · feed

9 Number crossword

Gleiche Zahlen sind gleiche Buchstaben.
Die angegebenen Lösungen helfen dir, das gesamte
Rätsel zu lösen. Alle Wörter sind in dieser Unit neu.

Wo im Rätsel findet man das englische Wort für ...

mischen	*9 across*
riesig	*i down*
zweimal	_____
einsam	_____
Medien	_____
Kumpel	_____
sich (etwas) vorstellen	_____
Nachricht	_____

New words ▶ p. 34

Ich mag ihn – er ist ein freundlicher **Typ**.	I like him – he's a friendly _____ .
Sein erster Tag im neuen Job ist **gut verlaufen**.	His first day in the new job _____ .
Gestern **träumte** ich **von** dir.	Yesterday I _____ you.
Er ist **nicht mehr** hier – er ist schon abgefahren.	He isn't here _____ – he's already left.
Wir mussten einen großen **Rucksack** packen.	We had to pack a big _____ .
Ich kann nicht weggehen – ich **erwarte** Besucher.	I can't go out – I'm _____ visitors.
Ich hatte kein Essen – **nicht einmal** ein Stück Brot.	I had no food – _____ a piece of bread.
Ihre Haare sind zu kurz für einen **Pferdeschwanz**.	Her hair is too short for a _____ .

10 The best word

Finde das Wort in der Strickleiter, das am besten in die Lücke passt.

empty   excited
exciting   clever

large   realistic
royal   strange

special   spicy
huge   sad

wet   huge
mild   personal

central   lonely
realistic   stupid

1 Here's some _exciting_ news. Mum's going to have another baby!

2 Open a window please. There's a _____ smell in the room.

3 Kim was very _____ because nobody came to visit her.

4 They live in a _____ house with 17 bedrooms.

5 Fantastic! That's a very _____ plan.

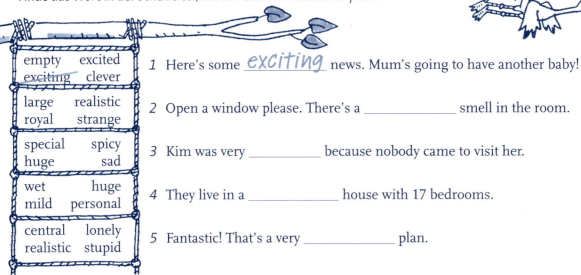

11 Word pairs

Welche Wörter passen zusammen?

ball
course
helmet
menu
message
recorder
rucksack
sound file

download, send, wear, pack, do, play, read, catch

message

New words ▸ p. 35

Ich bin **gekränkt**, weil du unhöflich zu mir warst.	I'm _____ because you were rude to me.
Es **kränkt** mich, wenn du unhöflich bist.	It _____ me when you're rude.
Könntest du bitte das Fernsehen **einschalten**?	Could you _____ the TV, please?
Ich bin **froh**, dass du dich besser fühlst.	I'm _____ you're feeling bettter.
die **Schönheit** der Berge Schottlands	the _____ of Scotland's mountains
Er **hat** mir wieder **Schimpfwörter nachgerufen**.	He _____ me _____ again.
Mutti **erlaubt** mir nicht, Make-up zu tragen.	Mum doesn't _____ me wear make-up.
Ich **würde** mich auf einer Insel einsam fühlen.	I _____ feel lonely on an island.
Sei nicht so aufgeregt. Entspann dich **einfach**!	Don't be so nervous. _____ relax!
Leider gibt's an jeder Schule einen **Schultyrannen**.	I'm afraid there's a _____ at every school.
Ich wollte nicht deine **Gefühle verletzen**.	I didn't want to hurt your _____ .
im Wörterbuch nach dem **Eintrag** suchen	look for the _____ in the dictionary
Was ist die **Übersetzung** diese Wortes?	What's the _____ of this word?
Kannst du dieses Wort ins Deutsche **übersetzen**?	Can you _____ this word into German?
eine falsche Antwort und eine **richtige** Antwort	a wrong answer and a _____ answer

12 Words with different meanings

Finde in der Liste die passenden Wörter zu den Paaren 1–7.
Trage sie ein und unterstreiche die deutschen Entsprechungen.

3
a) die Ankunftszeit im Fahrplan suchen
b) der Stundenplan für das neue Schuljahr

2
a) Vergiss nicht das Wechselgeld.
b) Wo müssen wir umsteigen?

a) Ist er ledig oder verheiratet?
b) eine einfache Fahrkarte kaufen

single **1**

5
a) Meine Eltern arbeiten in einer Fabrik.
b) Die Fahrstühle waren kaputt, aber jetzt funktionieren sie wieder.

4
a) die richtige Antwort
b) einen Fehler korrigieren

change
correct
timetable
single
work
walk

6
a) Lass uns zu Fuß gehen!
b) einen Spaziergang machen

2

New words ▸ pp. 38-42

Die Betonung liegt auf der dritten Silbe.	The _____ is on the third syllable.
eine **allgemeine Aussage**	a _____
Du hast **Glück** in dieser Mannschaft zu sein.	You _____ to be in this team.
Erzähle mir die guten **Nachrichten** zuerst.	First tell me the good _____ .
Kannst du meinen Namen **erraten**?	Can you _____ my name?
Türen **abschließen** und **aufschließen**	_____ and _____ doors
Muss ich den Knopf **drücken**?	Do I have to _____ the button?
Für seine **Rolle** im Film bekam er £2 **Millionen**.	He got £2 _____ for his _____ in the film.

13 Word search: town and country

Im Rätsel sind 18 „town and country"-Wörter versteckt.
Finde sie und übersetze sie ins Deutsche. (↓ →)

sea _____   Meer _____

H	H	A	R	B	O	U	R	V	P	B	S
I	T	O	W	E	R	F	S	F	A	R	M
L	D	S	Q	U	A	R	E	K	F	N	C
L	Y	E	Z	C	E	Z	A	R	W	P	R
B	M	L	A	A	B	I	S	L	A	N	D
E	O	A	W	N	R	O	A	D	T	Y	G
A	U	K	J	A	I	T	N	Y	G	I	H
C	N	E	F	L	D	U	Z	Y	Y	W	G
H	T	R	H	M	G	F	I	E	L	D	R
C	A	S	T	L	E	H	C	O	A	S	T
O	I	J	S	T	A	T	I	O	N	C	R
D	N	Z	O	D	R	B	A	Y	S	L	K

14 More about ... Orkney

Vervollständige den Text mit Wörtern vom Ticket.

Orkney is a group of _islands_ (1) ten miles from the Scottish coast. Today, about 20,000 people live _____ (2) 17 of the 70 islands. Most – about 15,000 – live on the _____ (3) island, Mainland. Between five _____ (4) 550 people live on the other islands. Hoy, the second largest island, has just under 300 people.

Orkney hasn't got many people, _____ (5) it has lots of schools – 21 for about 3,300 students. Some of the schools are very small – four of them have _____ (6) ten students.

When people travel from one island to _____ (7) they go by ferry, or fly between the bigger islands. The shortest flight is _____ (8) Westray and Papa Westray – it _____ (9) only two minutes.

Orkney is great _____ (10) holidays. If you go there, you can stay on a farm and learn how to _____ (11) cheese, enjoy the clean air and beautiful beaches and find out more about the 5,500 year _____ (12) of the people on the islands.

Ticket words: another, between, biggest, but, fewest, for, history, islands, make, on, takes, under

15 Lost words

Die fehlenden Wörter stecken im Maul des Hais. Finde sie und ergänze die Sätze.

1. The water here can be dangerous, so it's _unsafe_ to go swimming.
2. It's _____ to eat fruit and vegetables every day.
3. Jane's room is always in a mess – she's so _____ !
4. I think it's _____ if you don't do any sport.
5. Sue never laughs or smiles. She can't be a very _____ person.
6. Tim never says hello to anyone. Why is he so _____ ?
7. Which of you knows the _____ answer?
8. Jo was very _____ when he lost his favourite earring.
9. I'm _____ to hear that you aren't feeling well.

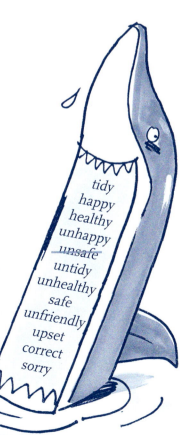

Shark words: tidy, happy, healthy, unhappy, unsafe, untidy, unhealthy, safe, unfriendly, upset, correct, sorry

New words ▸ pp. 44–47

Kannst du bitte das **Licht** einschalten?

Can you turn on the _____ , please?

Möchtest du **eine Tasse** Tee?

Would you like a _____ ?

In Großbritannien fährt **man** links.

In Great Britain _____ drive on the left.

Die **Schulversammlung** begann um 8.50.

_____ started at 8.50.

Der **Schulleiter** machte eine Ankündigung.

The _____ made an announcement.

Das kann nicht wahr sein – ich **glaube** es nicht.

That can't be true – I don't _____ it.

Ich bin bereit – wir können jetzt **beginnen**.

I'm ready – we can _____ now.

Es **könnte vielleicht** regnen – hast du eine Jacke?

It _____ rain – have you got a jacket?

Wenn es regnet, **könnten** wir ins Museum gehen.

If it rains, we _____ go to the museum.

Geh zum **Friseur** – deine Haare sind zu lang.

Go to the _____ – your hair's too long.

Ich bin nicht müde – warum **sollte** ich ins Bett?

I'm not tired – why _____ I go to bed?

Kannst du mir die Haare **schneiden**?

Can you _____ my hair?

Der Wind **blies** vom Westen.

The wind _____ from the west.

Er rannte schnell die Straße **hinüber**.

He ran quickly _____ the road.

Dieser **Anorak** ist schön warm.

This _____ is nice and warm.

Darf ich mit meinen Freunden sprechen?

_____ I _____ to talk to my friends?

Benutze ein **Mikrofon** – dann wirst du lauter.

Use a _____ – then you'll be louder.

Die Kirchen**glocke** läutet jede Stunde.

The church _____ rings every hour.

Das Schaf Dolly war ein berühmter **Klon**.

The sheep Dolly was a famous _____ .

Ist er **neidisch auf** meinen neuen Computer?

Is he _____ my new computer?

Mein Lieblings**gericht** ist Pommes und Bratwurst.

My favourite _____ is chips and sausage.

Ich brauche Fleisch und Gemüse für den **Eintopf**.

I need meat and vegetables for the _____ .

Die meisten Dörfer haben eine **Gemeindehalle**.

Most villages have a _____ .

ein Wort im Wörterbuch **nachschlagen**

_____ a word in the dictionary

die **Bedeutung** eines Wortes verstehen

_____ the meaning of a word

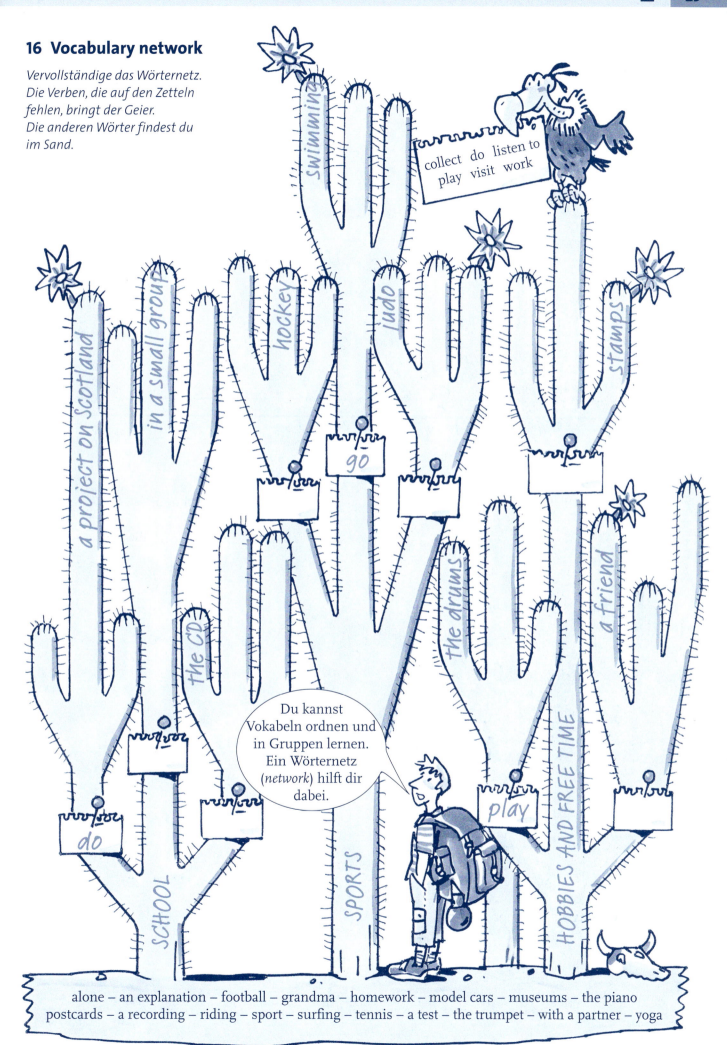

Unit 3

New words ▶ pp. 52–53

Hast du wirklich Karten für das **Endspiel**?	Have you really got tickets for the _____ ?
Leider wird dies sein **letztes** Spiel sein.	I'm afraid this will be his _____ game.
Er gewann das **Halbfinale**, verlor aber das Endspiel.	He won the _____ , but lost the final.
eine **Trainingseinheit** verpassen	miss a _____
Ich **interessiere mich für** Judo und Hockey.	I'_____ judo and hockey.
einen **Steckbrief** einer Person anschauen	look at a person's _____
Er verließ die Schule im **Alter** von 18.	He left school at the _____ of 18.
Welches **Geschlecht** hat das neue Baby?	What _____ is the new baby?
Mädchen sind **weiblich** und	Girls are _____
... Jungen sind **männlich**.	... and boys are _____ .
Der Bahnhof ist ein guter **Standort** für den Laden.	The station is a good _____ for the shop.

1 Words in pictures

a) Trage die angezeigten Körperteile ein.

1 _face_
2 _____
3 _____
4 _____
5 _____
6 _____
7 _____
8 _____
9 _____

b) Unterstreiche die beiden Wörter, die am besten zu den fettgedruckten Wörtern passen.

1 a broken / pretty / round **face**
2 blue / bright / loud **eyes**
3 a long / small / tidy **nose**
4 my left / medium / right **ear**
5 broken / careful / white **teeth**
6 grey / slow / tidy **hair**
7 a big / early / loud **mouth**
8 cheap / clean / strong **hands**

2 Hidden words

Ergänze die Wortgruppen, indem du Wörter mit Buchstaben der Wörter „training session" bildest.

3 Word families

a) *Finde die passenden Verben zu den angegebenen Nomen.*

1 arrival – **arrive**
2 beginning – _____
3 explanation – _____
4 feeling – _____
5 meaning – _____
6 mixture – _____
7 movement – _____
8 smoke – _____
9 phone – _____
10 practice – _____
11 bully – _____
12 invitation – _____
13 teacher – _____
14 translation – _____

b) *Vervollständige die Sätze mit einem Nomen oder einem Verb aus der Liste in a).*

1 What's the **meaning** (5) of this word? Can you _____ (3) it, please.

2 I've got an _____ (12) to Dan's party. – Really? Do you think he'll _____ me too?

3 How often do you _____ (10) the piano?

4 Please _____ (9) me and tell me when you _____ (1) at the station.

5 I read the book in English, but my little brother read the German _____ (14).

3

New words ▶ pp. 54–55

Er ist nicht **sportlich** – er bewegt sich nie.	He isn't very _____ – he never moves.
Unsere **Anhänger** kommen zu jedem Spiel.	Our _____ come to every match.
Viele Jugendliche **unterstützen** die Mannschaft.	Lots of teenagers _____ the team.
Versuch mal, den neuen Spieler zu **entdecken**.	Try and _____ the new player.
Die 22 Spieler sind schon auf dem Fußball**feld**.	The 22 players are already on the _____ .
In unserem Verein **trainieren** wir jeden Montag.	In our club we _____ every Monday.
Ein **Unentschieden** hilft uns nicht.	A _____ won't help us.
Das Spiel endete **2 beide**.	The game ended _____ .
Warum hat Smith kein **Tor geschossen**?	Why didn't Smith _____ ?
Nach 45 Minuten war der **Spielstand** 2:1.	After 45 minutes the _____ was 2:1.
Die Fans jubelten, als Black ein **Tor** schoss.	The fans cheered when Black scored a _____ .
Ist der **Trainer** böse auf seine Spieler?	Is the _____ angry with his players?
ein deutscher **Austauschschüler** in England	a German _____ in England
Klopfe, bevor du den Raum **betrittst**!	Knock before you _____ the room!
Ich war nicht da, als er kam. – **Schlechtes Timing**!	I was out when he came. – _____ !
Hungrig? – Nein, ich habe keinen **Appetit**.	Hungry? – No, I've got no _____ .
Die Fragen **beziehen** sich **auf** Seite 3.	The questions _____ page 3.

4 Word friends

In jedem Haus gibt es drei Wörter bzw. Wortverbindungen, die man direkt nach dem Verb auf der Fahne benutzen kann. Unterstreiche sie.

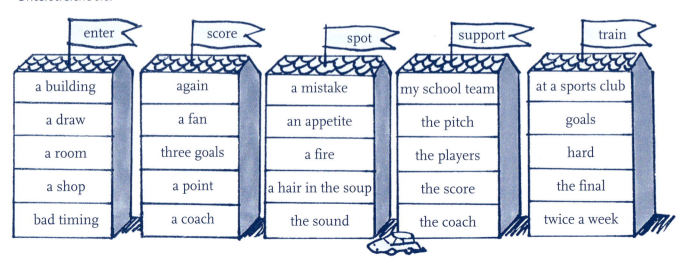

enter	score	spot	support	train
a building	again	a mistake	my school team	at a sports club
a draw	a fan	an appetite	the pitch	goals
a room	three goals	a fire	the players	hard
a shop	a point	a hair in the soup	the score	the final
bad timing	a coach	the sound	the coach	twice a week

5 The fourth word
Welches Wort wird hier gesucht?

1 one – two / once – _____
2 2:0 – two nil / 2:2 – two _____
3 man – male / woman – _____
4 students – teacher / players – _____
5 14 – age / female – _____
6 play – player / support – _____
7 close – lock / open – _____
8 Peter – name / 15 – _____

6 Verb forms
Ergänze die Tabelle der unregelmäßigen Verben.

1	do	did	done
2			beaten
3	break		
4		began	

5		cut	
6			fought
7	mean		
8	upset		

7 Definitions
Vervollständige die Definitionen mit Wörtern aus den Mauersteinen. Trage die richtigen Wörter aus der Sprühwolke in die rechte Spalte ein.

Cloud words: clone farmer final hairdresser head teacher supporter

Wall words: country hair looks last matches most person pigs school team washes winner

1 a person who *washes* and cuts other people's _____   *hairdresser*

2 a person who _____ like a copy of another _____   _____

3 a person who really likes a _____, wears team colours, goes to _____   _____

4 the _____ match – the _____ is the champion   _____

5 a person who works in the _____, often with cows, _____ etc.   _____

6 the _____ important teacher at a _____   _____

New words ▶ pp. 56–57

Die **ganze** Familie wird dieses Museum mögen.	The _____ family will love this museum.
ein **Künstler**, der Städte malt	an _____ who paints cities
Das Spiel beginnt um 20 Uhr im **Stadion**.	The match starts at 8 pm in the _____ .
Lass uns eine **Abmachung treffen**!	Let's _____ !
versuchen, einen Satz zu **umschreiben**	try to _____ a sentence
Ich habe eine **allgemeine** Frage zu Schottland.	I have a _____ question about Scotland.
Können wir diese Mannschaft **schlagen**?	Can we _____ this team?
einen **Pokal** gewinnen	win a _____
Es war ein fantastischer **Sieg** über United.	It was a fantastic _____ against United.
Am Ende waren wir die bessere Mannschaft.	_____ we were the better team.
Der Spielstand in der **Halbzeit** war 2:1.	The score at _____ was 2:1.
Es war ein toller **Schuss**, aber	It was a great _____ , but
... der **Torwart** hat den Ball gehalten.	... the _____ held the ball.

8 Word ladder

Gehe von unten nach oben, indem du bei jeder Sprosse einen Buchstaben veränderst.

luck — Good ★ in your English test tomorrow.

— Please close the windows and ★ them before you leave.

— I can't find my key. Can you help me ★ for it?

— prepare hot meals

— I ★ some photos with my new camera yesterday.

— How many pages are there in that ★ ?

— The English word for Fußballschuh is football ★.

— You can travel on water with this.

— Manchester United ★ Bayern Munich 2:1.

— ★ from a cow is called beef.

— Let's ★ tomorrow at 4 o'clock.

— one foot – two ★

— give food to an animal or person

need — The show is free, so we don't ★ any tickets.

9 Last letter – first letter

Der letzte Buchstabe von jedem Wort ist gleichzeitig der erste des nächsten Wortes.

1 Betonung
2 unterstützen
3 trainieren
4 Nachrichten
5 Hemd
6 reisen
7 Unterricht
8 Eintopf
9 Wörter
10 Schiff
11 Zeitungen
12 Stadion
13 Bedeutung
14 Torwart
15 wirklichkeitsnah

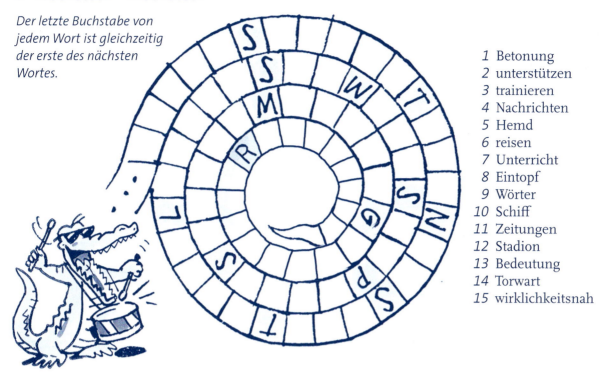

10 Pronunciation

Ordne die Wörter aus der Box der richtigen Aussprachegruppe zu.

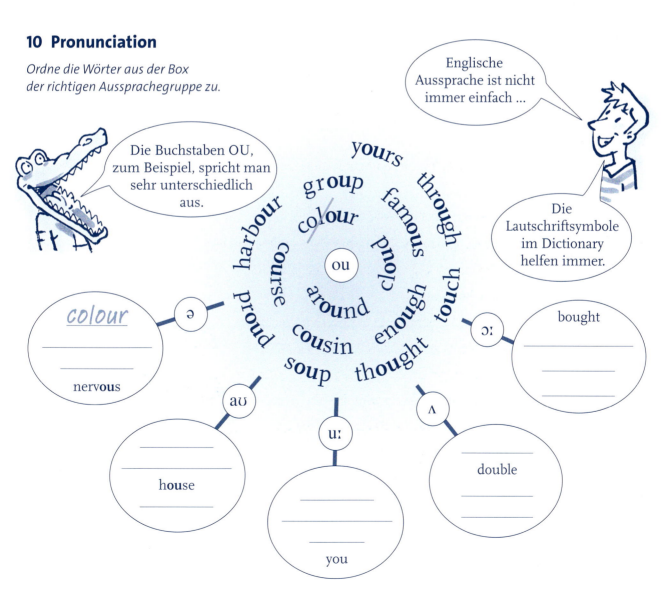

New words ▶ pp. 60–65

Die Suppe braucht noch etwas **Pfeffer**.   The soup needs some more _____ .

Ich meine, die Suppe braucht noch etwas **Salz**.   I think the soup needs some more _____ .

Kannst du das Essen und Trinken **organisieren**?   Can you _____ the food and drinks?

Wie **endete** die erste Halbzeit?   How did the first half _____ ?

Wir essen drei **Mahlzeiten** am Tag.   We eat three _____ a day.

Möchtest du **Reis** oder Kartoffeln zum Fleisch?   Would you like _____ or potatoes with the meat?

Schreibe einige Sätze **über dich selbst**.   Write some sentences _____ .

11 Crossword

Wörter, die im Deutschen zusammengeschrieben werden, schreibt man im Englischen häufig auseinander. Wie viele dieser Wörter findest du im Rätsel? Die dicken Striche helfen dir.

Across →
1 Badehose (8, 6)
5 Laufbahn (7, 5)
7 Spiel (5)
8 Sieg (3)
10 Tor (4)
14 Reitweg (6, 4)
17 Trainer/in (5)
18 Helm (6)
19 Endspiel (5)
21 Anhänger/in, Fan (9)

Down ↓
1 Schwimm-becken (8, 4)
2 Laufschuhe (7, 5)
3 Stadion (7)
4 Skipiste (3, 5)
6 Mannschaft (4)
9 Halbzeit (4)
11 Sporthalle (6, 4)
12 Sattel (6)
13 Torwart, Torfrau (10)
15 trainieren (5)
16 Spielfeld (5)
20 Pokal (3)

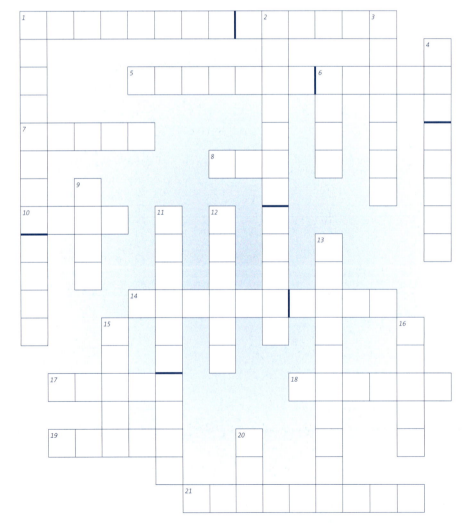

12 More about ... Manchester United

Vervollständige den Text mit den Wörtern aus der Box.

> ~~club~~   even   huge   learn
> match   millions   over   rich
> players   third   than   times

Manchester United is a famous English football <u>club</u>. They've been football champions of England 16 _____ and, in 1968, they were the first English club to win the European Cup. In 2008 they won it a _____ time. ManU isn't just popular in England. All _____ the world, the club has _____ of supporters. And it is very _____, so it has enough money to buy the best _____ (like Wayne Rooney or Cristiano Ronaldo). ManU's home is the _____ stadium at Old Trafford, with room for 75,000 fans to watch a _____. The club has _____ got a museum. More _____ 200,000 visitors go there every year to _____ about ManU's great past.

13 Hour glasses

Übersetze die Wörter und trage sie in die passende Sanduhr ein.

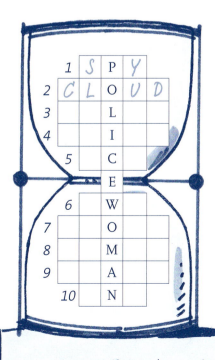

1 S P Y
2 C L O U D
3   L
4   I
5   C
     E
6 W
7 O
8 M
9 A
10 N

1 wer – Spion
2 Trainer – Wolke
3 Lineal – Preis, Gewinn
4 sich beeilen – Hemd
5 Eis – hinzufügen
6 Kugelschreiber – zwei
7 gekränkt – Spielstand
8 Aufsatz – römisch
9 Stahl – Zug
10 Schluss – Kunst

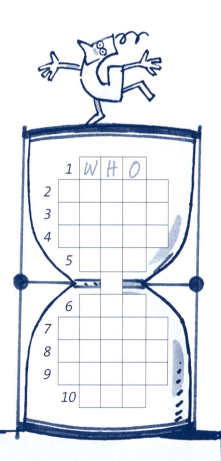

1 W H O
2
3
4
5
6
7
8
9
10

Das geheime Wort heißt: Englisch _____
                          Deutsch _____

New words ▸ p. 66; p. 104

Er war sehr **tapfer** – ein echter Held.	He was very _____ – a real hero.
Er stand auf und **machte** ein paar **Schritte**.	He stood up and _____ a few _____ .
Wir müssen noch nicht gehen – es ist **erst** 8 Uhr.	We don't have to go yet – it's _____ 8 am.
Papa ist in einer großen Familie **aufgewachsen**.	Dad _____ in a big family.
Jack schob den Rollstuhl **auf** die Fähre.	Jack pushed the wheelchair _____ the ferry.
Lass uns eine Boots**fahrt** auf dem See **machen**.	Let's _____ a boat _____ on the lake.
Guck! Sue hat ihren Pferdeschwanz **abgeschnitten**.	Look! Sue has _____ her ponytail.
Ein Unfall! Ruf einen **Krankenwagen**!	An accident! Call an _____ !
Bob ist Trainer für **Leichtathletik** und Schwimmen.	Bob's an _____ and swimming coach.
Der Sieger bekam eine Gold**medaille**.	The winner got a gold _____ .
Was sind deine **Hoffnungen** für die Zukunft?	What are your _____ for the future?
Fleißige Menschen bekommen gute Ergebnisse.	_____ people get good results.
Die Spieler mussten hart um den Titel **kämpfen**.	The players had to _____ hard _____ the title.
Die **Operation** hat ihm das Leben gerettet.	The _____ saved his life.
Sind diese Blumen **künstlich** oder echt?	Are these flowers _____ or real?
Er ist schon immer **verrückt auf** Fußball gewesen.	He has always been _____ football.
Schnee! Nun kann ich meinen **Schlitten** benutzen.	Snow! Now I can use my _____ .
Ich benutze den Rollstuhl, weil ich **behindert** bin.	I use the wheelchair because I'm _____ .
ein Spieler mit viel **Talent**.	a player with lots of _____
Wie oft hat sie England **vertreten**?	How often did she _____ England?

14 Odd word out
Finde und unterstreiche das Wort, das nicht passt.

1 lorry – ambulance – bus – journey

2 goalkeeper – ball – racket – bat

3 stadium – court – pool – bat

4 coach – player – semi-final – supporter

5 pizza – meal – hamburger – curry

6 appetite – breakast – lunch – dinner

7 medal – cup – pitch – prize

8 tennis – hope – football – hockey

3 **35**

15 Word search

Finde Wörter im Rätsel, um die Wortgruppen zu vervollständigen. (↓ →)

I	B	M	A	C	H	Q	P	A	R	A	L	Y	M	P	I	C	S
X	G	E	G	H	S	A	L	A	D	X	G	O	A	L	Z	W	E
G	C	D	L	A	H	A	S	O	F	A	T	D	C	M	E	E	T
Q	J	A	T	I	O	C	O	U	R	T	R	Y	M	V	O	Z	D
A	Y	L	G	R	E	K	L	A	M	P	A	G	S	K	I	S	A
S	H	A	M	B	U	R	G	E	R	M	I	F	E	T	D	S	T
H	E	G	B	S	T	A	D	I	U	M	N	E	W	A	U	J	H
O	O	M	E	O	T	R	A	M	L	H	E	R	K	X	O	S	L
R	M	T	D	P	U	L	L	O	V	E	R	R	Y	I	S	P	E
T	R	O	U	S	E	R	S	A	I	U	S	Y	T	N	C	A	T
S	C	U	P	B	O	A	R	D	W	Q	R	S	T	E	W	G	I
H	S	S	L	J	A	C	P	S	A	U	S	A	G	E	T	H	C
D	H	O	I	N	N	H	L	Y	K	P	I	Z	Z	A	A	E	S
S	I	C	V	S	O	I	A	G	P	S	H	E	L	F	B	T	G
K	P	K	A	O	R	P	N	S	L	O	R	R	Y	V	L	T	N
I	W	N	B	U	A	S	E	W	A	R	D	R	O	B	E	I	Q
R	I	T	U	P	K	A	U	N	D	E	R	G	R	O	U	N	D
T	P	H	S	T	V	O	L	L	E	Y	B	A	L	L	Q	N	P

transport

_____

_____

_____

_____

_____

_____

_____

_____

sport

athletics

_____

_____

_____

_____

_____

_____

room

_____

_____

_____

_____

_____

_____

_____

clothes

_____

_____

_____

_____

_____

_____

_____

food

_____

_____

_____

_____

_____

_____

_____

Unit 4

New words ▸ pp. 69

Ich mag keine Hotels, daher **gingen wir zelten**.	I don't like hotels, so we _____ .
Wir **zelteten** auf einem Feld.	We _____ in a field.
Lass uns auf diesem Fluss **Kanu fahren gehen**.	Let's _____ on this river.
Auf diesem Fluss habe ich gelernt, **Kanu zu fahren**.	I learned to _____ on this river.
Wir sind nicht alt genug, um **jagen** zu **gehen**.	We aren't old enough to _____ .
Ich kann nicht verstehen, warum sie Bären **jagen**.	I can't understand why they _____ bears.
im Winter **Schneeschuhwandern** gehen	_____ in winter
Schlafpartys im Haus eines Freundes **veranstalten**	_____ at a friend's house
Ich wollte nicht viel machen, nur **rumhängen**.	I didn't want to do much, just _____
Diese Band ist **beliebt bei** Kanadiern.	This band is _____ Canadians.
Wir wohnten in einer **Hütte** in den Bergen.	We stayed in a _____ in the mountains.
Der Bär ist tot. Warum haben sie ihn **erschossen**?	The bear's dead. Why did they _____ it?

1 Lost words

Ergänze die Sätze mit den Wörtern im Feuerwerk.

1 I was really surprised ___*at*___ the size of the Canadian forests.

2 ManU is playing _____ Liverpool FC today.

3 Jack is in hospital for an operation _____ his knee.

4 If you wait _____ Sue arrives, you'll be able to say hello.

5 It was cold in the garden so we went _____ and watched TV.

6 We live in the city centre, close _____ the big shops.

7 Mike was very upset _____ the bad news.

8 Anna moved her English books _____ a higher shelf.

9 There was no bridge at the river, so I couldn't get _____ .

10 Last night I dreamed _____ a holiday in Canada.

11 I didn't like the party at first, but _____ the end it was OK.

until at on against to about about in onto across inside

2 School words

Ergänze die fehlenden Wörter. Finde das „geheime Wort" und übersetze es.

1 b o a r d   Jack, can you write the answers on the ★ please?
2 _ _ _ _   We have lots of good singers in our school ★.
3 _ _ _ _ _ _   I'm in the seventh ★ this year.
4 _ _ _ _ _ _ _ _   How many ★ are there at your school? – About 800.
5 _ _ _ _ _ _ _   In ★ you learn about the past.
6 _ _ _ _ _ _ _   And in ★ you learn about flowers, animals, etc.
7 _ _ _ _ _ _   I need a ★, not a pen.
8 _ _ _ _ _ _ _   We have the same ★ for PE and English: Mr Hill.
9 _ _ _   In ★ you learn how to draw and paint.
10 _ _ _ _   In English we have to write an ★ about our hobbies.

The secret word is: Englisch _____   Deutsch _____

3 Word pairs

Welche Wörter passen zusammen?

New words ▸ pp. 70 – 71

Ich hoffe, **Mama** und Papa werden kommen.	I hope _____ and dad will come.
Er **beschwerte** sich **über** die kalte Suppe.	He _____ about the cold soup.
Die Musik ist OK, aber ich hasse den **Liedtext**.	The song sounds OK, but I hate the _____ .
Könntest du diese **Rechnung** für mich bezahlen?	Could you pay this _____ for me?
Es ist nicht meine Schuld, dass du kein Buch hast.	_____ that you don't have a book.
Unsere Eltern sind **streng**, aber fair.	Our parents are _____ , but fair.
Vielleicht hast du **beim** Test gut **abgeschnitten**.	Maybe you _____ the test.
Ich kann nicht kommen. Ich **habe Hausarrest**.	I can't come. I _____ .
Der neue Tag beginnt um **Mitternacht**.	The new day begins at _____ .
Dieser **altmodischer** Hut gehörte Opa.	This _____ hat was grandpa's.
Ich mag **moderne** Städte lieber als alte Städte.	I like _____ cities more than old cities.
ein **lockerer** Typ, der nie wütend wird	an _____ type who never gets angry
Dieser Lärm **geht mir** wirklich **auf die Nerven**!	This noise is really _____ !
Ärgert es dich, wenn du Dinge verlierst?	Does it _____ you when you lose things?
Kommt **Leute** – lasst uns nach Hause gehen.	Come on _____ – let's go home.
Ich muss **bis spätestens** 8 Uhr zu Hause sein.	I have to be home _____ eight o'clock.
Bitte **brainstormt** so viele Ideen wie möglich.	Please _____ as many ideas as possible.

4 One or two letters?

Trage die fehlenden Buchstaben ein:
g oder **gg**, **l** oder **ll**, usw.

g/gg re_gg_ae, be____in, lan____uage, bi____est, fo____, fo____y

l/ll co____ect, adu____t, unti____, ta____ent, mode____, pu____over

m/mm co____unity, swi____er, wo____an, gra____ar, mo____ent, thermo____eter

p/pp re____ort, sho____ing, pe____er, su____orter, re____resent, disa____ear

r/rr dia____y, ma____ied, guita____, ti____ed, hu____y, diffe____ent

s/ss promi____e, e____ay, gla____es, gue____, hu____band, i____land

t/tt bo____le, wa____er, pre____y, wea____her, spaghe____i

5 Vocabulary network

Vervollständige das Wörternetz. Die Verben, die auf den Zetteln fehlen, bringt der Geier. Die anderen Wörter findest du im Sand.

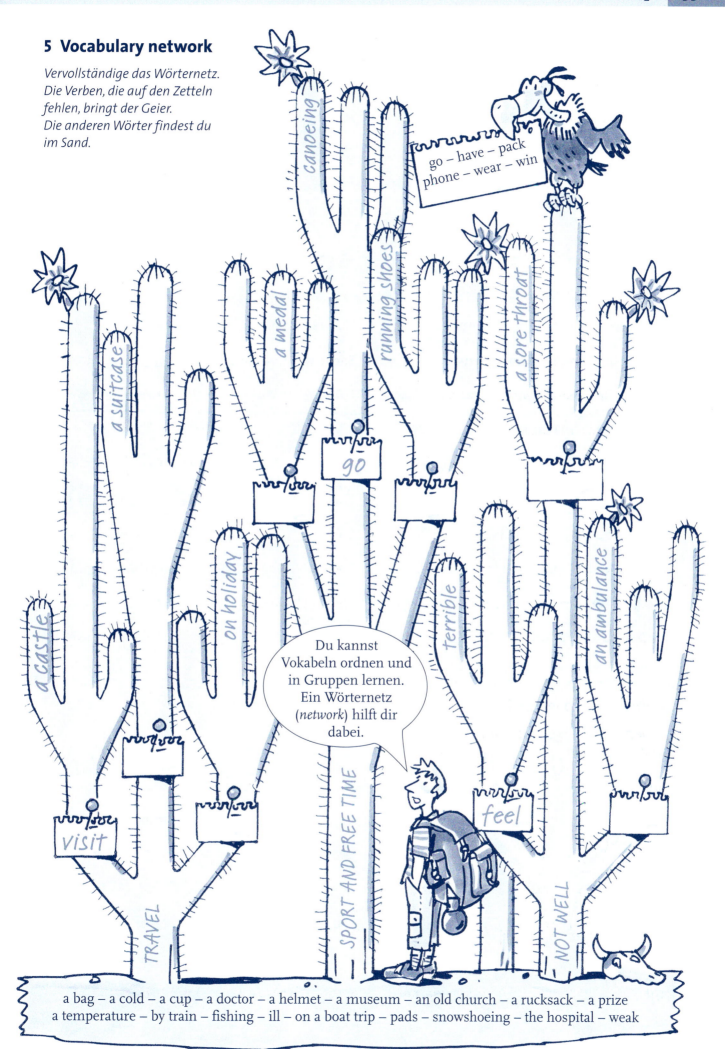

40 | 4

New words ▸ pp. 72 – 73

Ist Ontario die größte **Provinz** Kanadas?	Is Ontario Canada's largest _____?
Ist diese Musik **traditionell** oder modern?	Is this music _____ or modern?
Wir müssen uns gegen Diebe **schützen**.	We must _____ ourselves against thieves.
Haben viele Menschen den **Angriff** überlebt?	Did many people survive the _____?
Warum **greifen** Bären Menschen **an**?	Why do bears _____ people?
Der Zug fährt um **genau** 18 Uhr ab.	The train leaves at _____ 6 pm.
Es gibt keine gute **Begründung** für die Jagd.	There's no good _____ for hunting.
Gib mir nicht **die Schuld** für deine Fehler!	Don't _____ me for your mistakes!
gute **Argumente** in einer Diskussion **vorbringen**	_____ good _____ in a discussion
Tim stimmt mir zu, aber Jo **ist anderer Meinung**.	Tim agrees with me, but Jo _____ .
Wer ist der **Leiter** dieser Gruppe?	Who's the _____ of this group?
Wir kennen **uns** – wir sind alte Freunde.	We know _____ – we're old friends.
Die **Bühne** ist zu klein für so viele Schauspieler.	The _____ is too small for so many actors.
eine gute **Mischung** von alten und neuen Liedern	a good _____ of old and new songs
Lass uns den **Refrain** zusammensingen.	Let's sing the _____ together.

6 Spot the mistakes

In jedem Satz sind zwei Fehler.
Unterstreiche und korrigiere sie.

1 When <u>childs</u> are young they often has teddy bears.   *children* _____

2 Bears can look realy sweet and lots off people love them.   _____   _____

3 But they are allso large and very danger animals.   _____   _____

4 They usualy hunt at night or in the errly morning.   _____   _____

5 Bears can ran quickly and they are great swimers.   _____   _____

6 It's very interresting to watch how a bear catches salmons.   _____   _____

7 It stand in the river and waits quitely for a long time.   _____   _____

8 When the bare sees a fish it jump and catches it.   _____   _____

7 Word search

Im Rätsel sind 28 Tiere versteckt.
Finde und schreibe sie auf. (↓ →)

hedgehog

L	S	J	E	C	G	H	E	D	G	E	H	O	G	C
I	Q	F	L	H	I	O	V	X	R	S	N	A	K	E
O	U	O	E	I	R	M	H	M	H	T	M	N	X	S
N	I	X	P	C	A	O	O	A	I	S	B	H	R	C
S	R	F	H	K	F	U	R	I	N	E	S	C	O	F
H	R	X	A	E	F	S	S	M	O	N	K	E	Y	Y
E	E	Z	N	N	E	E	E	C	Y	W	A	E	S	U
E	L	K	T	P	I	G	K	K	Z	I	N	H	A	G
P	F	F	S	B	O	B	C	Y	A	B	G	A	L	B
Q	R	T	N	Y	S	E	S	L	D	P	A	M	M	U
Y	O	U	G	F	X	A	M	O	L	E	R	S	O	D
P	G	R	C	O	W	R	P	A	R	R	O	T	N	G
V	Z	K	G	O	F	P	H	I	P	P	O	E	K	I
K	X	E	C	R	O	C	O	D	I	L	E	R	W	E
X	H	Y	G	R	A	B	B	I	T	I	G	E	R	Y

8 Pronunciation

In jeder Wortgruppe gibt es bei zwei Wörtern stumme Buchstaben. Finde die Wörter und streiche die stummen Buchstaben durch.

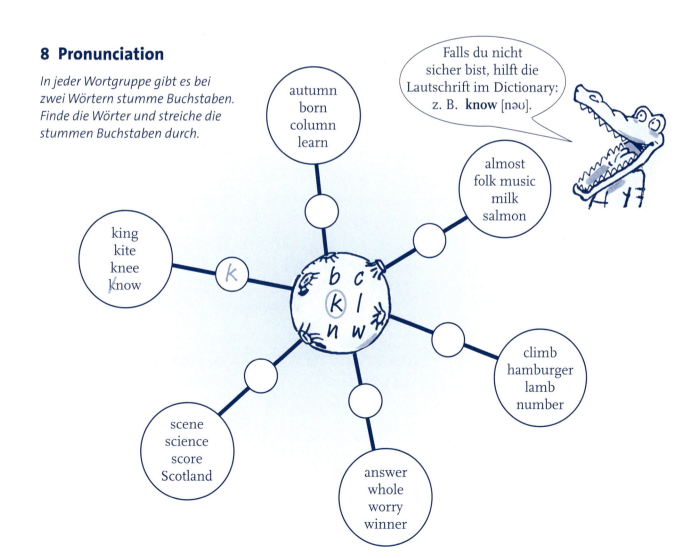

4

New words ▶ *pp. 76 – 80*

Über 10 **Prozent** der Briten leben in London.	Over 10 _____ of the British live in London.
Die Zimmer kosten 50 Euro **pro** Nacht.	The rooms cost 50 euros _____ night.
Der See ist 14 **Kilometer** lang.	The lake ist 14 _____ long.
Ein Meter hat 100 **Zentimeter**.	There are 100 _____ in a metre.
ein 30 **Kilogramm** schwerer Hund	a 30-_____ dog
Er ist 13, aber sieht aus wie ein **Fünfzehnjähriger**.	He's 13, but looks like a _____ .
Sie hat einen **vierzehnjährige** Sohn.	She's got a _____ son.
Hotelgäste mögen die **entspannte** Atmosphäre.	Hotel guests like the _____ atmosphere.
Es ist **verrückt**, im Winter nur ein T-Shirt zu tragen.	It's _____ to wear just a T-shirt in winter.
Wolltest du nicht deinen Aufsatz **überarbeiten**?	Didn't you want to _____ your essay?
die **Rechtschreibung** in einem Aufsatz überprüfen	check the _____ in an essay
für mehr Geld **streiken**	go on _____ for more money

9 Words with different meanings

Finde in der Liste die passenden Wörter zu den Paaren 1–7.
Trage sie ein und unterstreiche die deutschen Entsprechungen.

3
a) Der Zug fährt um 17.30 ab.
b) Wir trainieren dreimal die Woche.

2
a) ein Bild ausmalen
b) eine schöne Farbe

a) auf der Nordseite des Platzes
b) 20 Quadratmeter

square

1

5
a) Ich gehe einmal pro Woche schwimmen.
b) Kinder mussten einst in Fabriken arbeiten.

4
a) Was für ein Datum haben wir heute?
b) Kim hat eine Verabredung mit Alex.

argument
colour
date
final
once
square
train

a) das Endspiel
b) die letzte Minute

6

7
a) ein böser Streit
b) eine gute Begründung

10 Odd word out

Finde und unterstreiche das Wort, das nicht passt.

1 kilometre – minute – metre – centimetre

2 lyrics – drawing – photo – picture

3 seven – per cent – eight – nine

4 lyrics – music – text message – song

5 eyes – build – glasses – see

6 adults – children – teenagers – sledges

7 shop – gig – supermarket – department store

8 journey – ride – trip – coast

11 The fourth word

Welches Wort fehlt hier?

1 one – thousand / metre – _____

2 skate – skater / play – _____

3 he – they / himself – _____

4 green – colour / two – _____

5 parrot – bird / piano – _____

6 days – month / months – _____

7 day – sun / night – _____

8 man – men / knife – _____

12 More about … traditional Inuit hunting

Vervollständige den Text mit Wörtern aus der Box.

The Inuit live in Greenland and in the north of Canada, where winter *temperatures* (1) can be minus 40 degrees Celsius. So it's _____ (2) too cold to have farm animals or to grow food. That's why hunting and _____ (3) were once a very big part of Inuit life. The meat of sea animals like the walrus or the whale, or of _____ (4) animals like the polar bear, was traditional Inuit food. And of course, hunting wasn't _____ (5) important for food. The Inuit could also use animal *skins to make clothes. In the past, when the Inuit hunted sea animals they used a *kayak*, a _____ (6) of canoe. And on land they _____ (7) sledges with dogs. A team of dogs could easily pull 20 kilos. And dogs _____ (8) smell very well too, so they could help the Inuit to find the animals. Sometimes a hunting trip took a few days, so the Inuit often _____ (9) little igloos when they needed a place to sleep at night. Inside an igloo, the temperature could be _____ (10) 20 degrees Celsius when it was only minus 40 outside.

about   built   could
fishing   just   kind
land   much
temperatures   used

4

New words ▸ pp. 81–82

mit **Messer** und Gabel essen	eat with a _____ and fork
Hat jemand angerufen, **während** ich weg war?	Did anybody phone _____ I was out?
Wir müssen sie vor den Gefahren **warnen**.	We have to _____ them about the dangers.
Kann man Bären in diesem **Wald** sehen?	Can you see bears in these _____?
Wir brauchen **Holz** für das Feuer.	We need some _____ for the fire.
Die Polizei kannte das **Opfer** nicht.	The police didn't know the _____.
Schicke Jugendliche tragen oft die **neueste** Mode.	Trendy teens often wear the _____ fashion.
Es gab ein Feuer, aber wir konnten **entkommen**.	There was a fire, but we were able to _____.
Wo kann ich lernen, mit einem Kanu zu **paddeln**?	Where can I learn to _____ a canoe?
Diese **Stromschnellen** sind für Boote gefährlich.	These _____ are dangerous for boats.

13 Number crossword

*Gleiche Zahlen sind gleiche Buchstaben.
Die angegebenen Lösungen helfen dir,
das gesamte Rätsel zu lösen.
Alle Wörter sind in dieser Unit neu.*

Crossword grid with filled letters: a-across: LATEST; g-down: POPULAR

Wo im Rätsel findet man das englische Wort für …

Provinz	e across
Mikrophon	o down
beliebt	_____
streng	_____
Erwachsene(r)	_____
Streit	_____
Messer	_____
ärgern	_____

14 Word groups

Trage die Wörter aus der Wolke in die richtigen Sterne ein.

actor – choir – chorus – cleaner – cloudy – concert – farmer – fog – instrument – lyrics
painter – platforms – railway – rain – shop assistant – snow – song – stormy
suitcases – sunny – ticket machines – timetable – toilets – trains – tornado – waiter

15 Opposites

Trage die Gegenteile der fettgedruckten Wörter in die Lücken ein.

1 have **easy-going** / _strict_ parents

2 Do you really **agree** / _____ with me?

3 wear **old-fashioned** / _____ clothes

4 turn the radio **on** / _____

5 **over** / _____ 20 per cent

6 **enter** / _____ the classroom

7 at the **top** / _____ of the shelf

8 **forget** / _____ an important date

9 There are 90 **arrivals** / _____ every day.

10 find a **husband** / _____

11 an **exciting** / a _____ film

12 a really **hot** / _____ day

13 a **clean** / _____ city

14 Wait **downstairs** / _____ in your room!

Unit 5

New words ▸ pp. 88–89

Wann werden sie die Gewinner **bekanntgeben**?	When will they _____ the winners?
Das musst du selbst entscheiden.	_____
Diese Zeitung hat einen tollen Sport**teil**.	This paper has a great sport _____ .
Ein **Redakteur** überprüft und korrigiert Texte.	An _____ checks and corrects texts.
Amerikanische **Filme** im Fernsehen anschauen	watch American _____ on TV
Was **produziert** diese Fabrik?	What does this factory _____ ?
Hast du diesen **Artikel** noch nicht gelesen?	Haven't you read this _____ yet?
Wer wird den Bericht **veröffentlichen**?	Who's going to _____ the report?
Wir können ein Foto oder eine **Zeichnung** benutzen.	We can use a photo or a _____ .
Als erstes musst du eine Linie **zeichnen**.	First you have to _____ a line.
Unser Wohltätigkeitsbasar war wieder ein **Erfolg**.	Our jumble sale was a _____ again.
Erfolgreiche Schriftsteller verkaufen viele Bücher.	_____ writers sell lots of books.
Ich trage **Kopfhörer**, wenn ich Musik spiele.	I wear _____ when I play music.
Wie groß ist dein Computerbildschirm?	How big is your computer _____ ?

1 Pronunciation

Ordne die Wörter aus der Box der richtigen Aussprachegruppe zu.

ʊ juː ʌ

bully but computer community excuse full fun huge menu
publish pull push put sugar summer tunnel tube trumpet

bully	computer	fun
_____	_____	_____
_____	_____	_____
_____	_____	_____
_____	_____	_____
_____	_____	_____

2 Last letter – first letter

Der letzte Buchstabe von jedem Wort ist gleichzeitig der erste des nächsten Wortes.

1 Refrain
2 Erfolg
3 erfolgreich
4 Leiter, Führer
5 Stromschnellen
6 Schreibung, Schreibweise
7 Oma
8 ankündigen
9 Redakteur
10 überarbeiten, wiederholen
11 elektrisch
12 Currygericht
13 ja
14 Abschnitt

3 Word families

Finde die passenden Verben zu den angegebenen Nomen.

1 announcement – *announce*

2 revision – _____

3 spelling – _____

4 drawing – _____

5 ending – _____

6 life – _____

7 attack – _____

8 supporter – _____

9 recording – _____

10 laughter – _____

4 Making phrases

Vervollständige die Audrücke mit einem Verb von den Zetteln.

1 *turn* _____ on the radio

2 _____ people about the bears in the forest

3 _____ what you read in the newspaper

4 _____ with my partner's ideas

5 _____ up in a big city

6 _____ up a word I don't know

7 _____ from a fire in a hotel

5

New words ▶ p. 90

Überfliegt den Text, aber lest ihn nicht in Detail.	_____ the text, but don't read it in detail.
die **Biographie** einer berühmten Person lesen	read the _____ of a famous person
Gute Broschüren haben **nützliche** Informationen.	Good brochures have _____ information.
Ich benutze **Fettdruck** für **Bildunterschriften**.	I use _____ for _____ .
Wann bist du heute Morgen **aufgewacht**?	When did you _____ this morning?
Bitte **wecke** mich morgen um sieben Uhr.	Please _____ me tomorrow at o'clock.
Ich brauche **Stille**, **damit** ich lesen kann.	I need _____ I can read.

5 The fourth word

Welches Wort wird hier gesucht?

1 banana – fruit / pea – _____

2 lunch – meal / chicken curry – _____

3 salmon – fish / woodpecker – _____

4 Friday – day / August – _____

5 dishwasher – machine / piano – _____

6 Britain – island / Uranus – _____

7 seven – number / pink – _____

8 song – music / drawing – _____

6 Definitions

Vervollständige die Definitionen mit Wörtern aus den Mauersteinen. Trage die richtigen Wörter aus Kens Zeitung in die rechte Spalte ein.

drawing
editor
headphones

strike
silence
sleepover

	corrects	everybody	ears	home	picture		
	more	noise	pen	radio	spend	texts	work	

1 Wear these over your *ears* to listen to an mp3 player or the _____ .   *headphones*

2 when people stop _____ because they want _____ money   _____

3 when you _____ the night at a friend's _____   _____

4 someone who checks and _____ articles and other _____   _____

5 a _____ that you make with a pencil or _____   _____

6 when _____ is quiet and there is no _____   _____

7 Hour glasses

Übersetze die Wörter und trage sie in die passende Sanduhr ein.

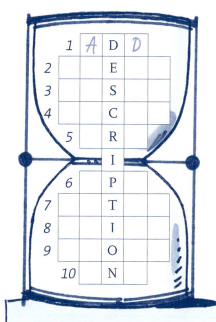
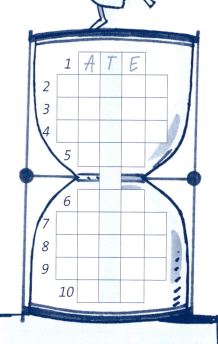

1. aß – hinzufügen
2. Königin – schmutzig
3. aufgebracht – Strand
4. Medaille – Tatsachen
5. versuchen – Kind
6. Mülltonne – Spion
7. Chor – bis
8. Endspiel – ruhig
9. Beweis – Bühne
10. Schluss – krank

Das geheime Wort in der rechten Sanduhr heißt: Englisch _____

Deutsch _____

8 Word ladder

Gehe von unten nach oben, indem du bei jeder Sprosse einen Buchstaben veränderst.

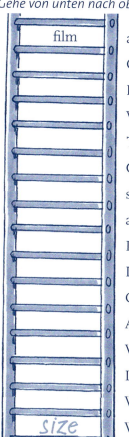

- film — another word for movie
- Click here to download the sound ★.
- I was ill last week but I'm ★ again now.
- Which underground ★ goes to St Paul's Cathedral?
- This isn't my bag – ★ is blue, not black.
- Germany – kilometre / Britain and America – ★
- she – female / he – ★
- a small black animal that lives under the ground
- I lost some money because there was a ★ in my pocket.
- Did you get a ★ in the school play?
- Can you explain this grammar ★, please?
- A ★ person is unfriendly to other people.
- When did you learn to ★ a horse?
- Let's ★ behind this wall. Then nobody will see us.
- Which ★ of the street is number 47?
- size — What ★ is this T-shirt? Medium or large?

5

New words ▶ p. 91

Wir fanden keine Antwort auf das **Rätsel**.	We didn't find an answer to the _____.
Er trägt eine schwarze **Leder**jacke.	He's wearing a black _____ jacket.
Kirchenorgeln haben sehr viele **Pfeifen**.	Church organs have got lots of _____.
Eine Flasche **ragte aus** der Einkaufstasche **heraus**.	A bottle _____ of the shopping bag.
Fleisch muss man im Kühlschrank **aufbewahren**.	You have to _____ meat in the fridge.
Er **drückte** ihre Hand und lächelte.	He _____ her hand and smiled.
Bist du auch **gut in** Französisch?	Are you _____ French too?
Wann wurde diese CD **auf den Markt gebracht**?	When was this CD _____?
Es tut mir Leid, aber die Karten sind **ausverkauft**.	I'm sorry, but the tickets are _____.

9 Word building

Verbinde ein Wort aus den Steinen mit einem Wort aus der Liste. Trage die deutsche Übersetzung ein.

Eine Regel gibt es leider nicht. Also merkt euch die Einzelfälle!

Wenn man Wörter miteinander verbindet, schreibt man sie mal auseinander, mal mit Bindestrich, mal zusammen.

bold, text, running, snow, class, great, semi, chat, car, wheel

1 _bold_ print   _Fettdruck_
2 _____ park   _____
3 _____ room   _____
4 _____ shoes _____
5 _____ message _____

6 _semi-_ final   _____
7 _____ grandfather _____
8 _class_ room   _____
9 _____ shoes _____
10 _____ chair _____

10 Odd word out

Finde und unterstreiche das Wort, das nicht passt.

1 photo – racket – drawing – picture
2 stadium – article – report – story
3 read – score – skim – scan
4 announce – report – skate – tell

5 felt tip – pen – pencil – pipe
6 salad – sandwich – silence – strawberry
7 leather – monitor – stone – wood
8 e-mail – instant message – puzzle – text message

11 Words in pictures: Fruit and vegetables

a) Wie heißt das abgebildete Obst und Gemüse?
Trage die Wörter in die nummerierten Lücken ein.

1 bright long red   *tomatoes* _____

2 delicious windy forest _____

3 sweet Spanish spicy _____

4 short hard green _____

5 big grey garden _____

6 delicious German neat _____

7 bright round orange _____

8 healthy green empty _____

9 delicious sunny new _____

10 long yellow German _____

b) 2 von 3 Adjektiven passen zu den Wörtern, die du eingetragen hast. Unterstreiche sie.

12 Opposites

Trage die Gegenteile der fett gedruckten Wörter in die Lücken ein.

1 the **best** / _____ book I've ever read

2 be **good** / _____ at French

3 at the **bottom** / _____ of the street

4 **bright** / _____ colours

5 a **healthy** / an _____ meal

6 **modern** / _____ furniture

7 arrive **early** / _____ for the lesson

8 a **tidy** / an _____ room

9 **in front of** / _____ the house

10 a good **question** / _____

11 **silence** / _____

12 ask about **departure** / _____ times

13 look **left** / _____

14 **remember** / _____ to phone a friend

New words ▸ pp. 92–93

Wie lang sind die Sommer**ferien** in Kanada?	How long is summer _____ in Canada?
ein Projekt **auf den Weg bringen**	_____ a project _____
Ich glaube, Alex ist in Chris **verknallt**.	I think Alex _____ Chris.
400 Meilen! Ist die Fahrt wirklich **so** lang?	400 miles! Is the journey really _____ long?
Der März ist der Monat, den ich **am wenigsten** mag!	March is the month I like _____ !
Hab ich dir schon unser Foto**album** gezeigt?	Have I showed you our photo _____ yet?
In Schottland hört man oft den **Dudelsack**.	You often hear the _____ in Scotland.
Was ist deine Traum**karriere**?	What's you dream _____ ?
Ich möchte ein **Musiker** in einer Band werden.	I'd like to be a _____ in a band.
Wir können in ein Konzert oder in die **Oper** gehen.	We can go to a concert or to the _____ .
Ich habe viele CDs, aber keine **Schallplatten**.	I have lots of CDs, but no _____ .
Hast du ihre neue **Single** schon gehört?	Have you heard their new _____ yet?
Passt die **Melodie** wirklich zum Songtext?	Does the _____ really go with the lyrics?
Wie viele **Titel** gibts auf der CD?	How many _____ are there on the CD?

13 The best word

Finde das Wort in der Strickleiter, das am besten in die Lücke passt.

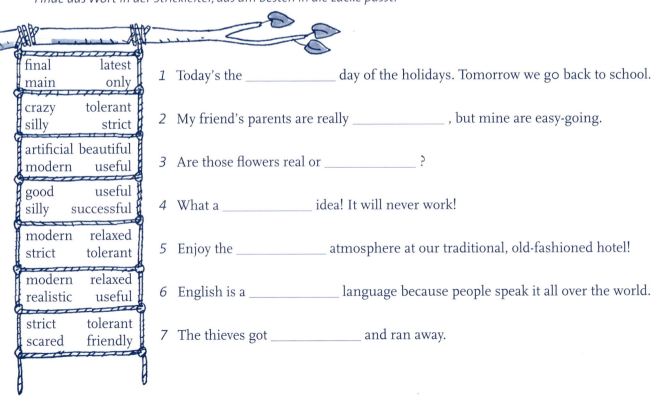

1 Today's the _____ day of the holidays. Tomorrow we go back to school.

2 My friend's parents are really _____ , but mine are easy-going.

3 Are those flowers real or _____ ?

4 What a _____ idea! It will never work!

5 Enjoy the _____ atmosphere at our traditional, old-fashioned hotel!

6 English is a _____ language because people speak it all over the world.

7 The thieves got _____ and ran away.

14 Hidden words

Ergänze die Wortgruppen, indem du Wörter mit Buchstaben der Wörter „musical instruments" bildest.

musical instruments = Musikinstrumente

15 Word search - The media

15 englische Begriffe aus dem Wortfeld „Medien" sind im Rätsel versteckt.
Finde sie und übersetze sie ins Deutsche. (↓ →)

E	Z	M	O	N	I	T	O	R	H	P	C
D	M	A	G	A	Z	I	N	E	E	U	Q
I	K	Z	W	B	H	X	N	N	A	B	T
T	O	J	E	O	P	R	A	E	D	L	M
O	R	E	C	O	R	D	R	W	P	I	O
R	H	V	D	K	O	R	T	S	H	S	B
Y	E	L	Z	S	G	E	I	P	O	H	I
G	F	R	T	U	R	P	C	A	N	X	L
R	A	D	I	O	A	O	L	P	E	B	E
N	Z	D	G	K	M	R	E	E	S	G	H
W	N	E	W	S	M	T	Q	R	D	V	W
S	U	T	E	L	E	V	I	S	I	O	N

monitor - Bildschirm

New words ▸ pp. 95–96

Wie viele Menschen arbeiten für diese **Firma**?	How many people work for this _____ ?
Kann ich ein **Exemplar** des Berichts haben?	Can I have a _____ of the report?
Nenne mir eine Farbe, **zum Beispiel** rot.	Give me a colour, red _____ .
Fangen Nomen mit **Großbuchstaben** an?	Do nouns start with _____ ?
Ist simple past hier die richtige **Zeit**?	Is simple past the right _____ here?

16 Word friends

Welche Wörter auf den Steinen passen in die Lücken?

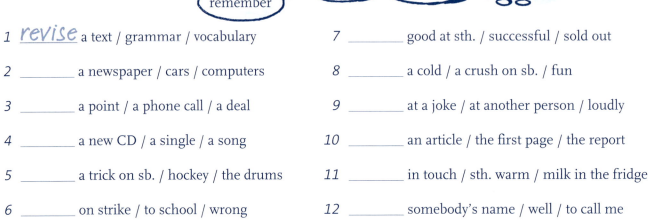

Stones: keep, revise, make, record, produce, play, be, laugh, go, have, skim, remember

1 **revise** a text / grammar / vocabulary
2 _____ a newspaper / cars / computers
3 _____ a point / a phone call / a deal
4 _____ a new CD / a single / a song
5 _____ a trick on sb. / hockey / the drums
6 _____ on strike / to school / wrong
7 _____ good at sth. / successful / sold out
8 _____ a cold / a crush on sb. / fun
9 _____ at a joke / at another person / loudly
10 _____ an article / the first page / the report
11 _____ in touch / sth. warm / milk in the fridge
12 _____ somebody's name / well / to call me

17 Scrambled words: American and British English

Die Buchstabenrätsel ergeben Wörter aus dem amerikanischen Englisch. Trage diese und ihre britischen Entsprechungen ein. Die Tipps helfen dir.

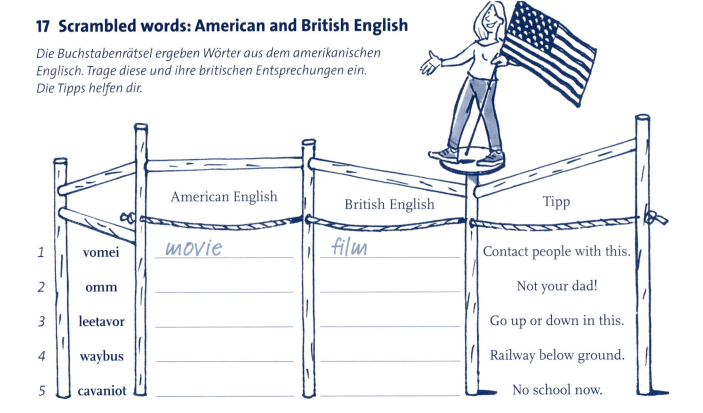

		American English	British English	Tipp
1	vomei	movie	film	Contact people with this.
2	omm			Not your dad!
3	leetavor			Go up or down in this.
4	waybus			Railway below ground.
5	cavaniot			No school now.

18 Crossword

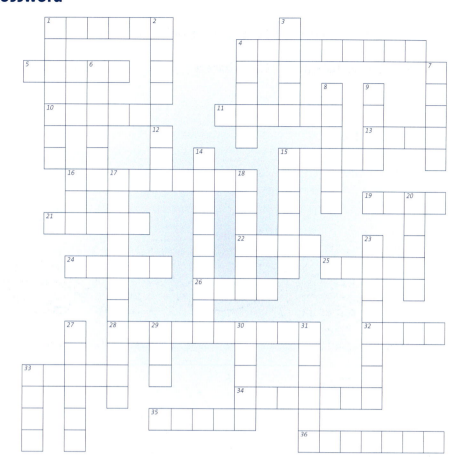

Across

1 A cathedral is a kind of ★. (6)
4 the story of a somebody's life (9)
5 You need it to cut bread. (5)
10 The name of the planet we live on. (5)
11 opposite of 'old-fashioned' (6)
13 a name for the underground in London (4)
15 Somebody stole my bike ★ I was in the shop. (5)
16 In this sport, you run, jump, etc. (9)
19 You need it when you play hockey, tennis, etc. (4)
21 oranges, apples, bananas, etc. (9)
22 60 minutes – an hour / 30 minutes – ★ an hour (4)
24 newspapers, magazines, radio, TV, the internet, etc. (5)
25 a person who trains a sports team (5)
26 the person at work who tells you what you have to do (4)
28 friend – friendly / success – ★ (10)
32 from all ★ England = from every part of England (4)
33 one – once / two – ★ (5)
34 the main city in a country (7)
35 not very clever; stupid (5)
36 a building where you can watch a football match (7)

Down

1 when people play music for an audience (7)
2 very, very big (4)
3 another word for 'film' (5)
4 I like ★ and eggs for breakfast (5)
6 opposite of 'remember' (6)
7 The wife of a king is a ★. (5)
8 opposite of 'beginning' (6)
9 another word for 'friend' (4)
12 I'm 14. What ★ are you? (3)
14 This gives you information about when buses, trains, etc. arrive and leave. (9)
15 They're round. A car has got four of them. (6)
16 We need it to live. (3)
17 a person who washes and cuts hair (11)
18 the things that tourists like to see (6)
20 Can you turn on the ★ ? It's so dark here. (5)
23 October 3rd is a ★ holiday in Germany (8)
27 a person who checks and corrects texts (6)
29 A team that wins a final often gets this prize. (3)
30 opposite of 'mild' (5)
31 the words of a song (6)
33 make – made / take – ★ (4)

Lösungen

1

Introduction

1 Lost words
1 In, *2* of, *3* from, *4* to, *5* at, *6* by,
7 before, *8* between

2 Verb forms
2 show – showed – shown
3 spend – spent – spent
4 hide – hid – hidden
5 do – did – done
6 take – took – taken
7 fly – flew – flown
8 read – read – read
9 throw – threw – thrown
10 speak – spoke – spoken
11 write – wrote – written
12 ride – rode – ridden

3 Crossword

¹D		²P	R	A	C	T	I	³S	E	
R		I						I		
⁴G	U	I	T	A	R		⁵B	A	N	D
M		N			⁶F			N		
	⁷P	R	O	G	R	A	M	M	E	R
		L			N			E		
⁸S	T	A	R	⁹F			¹⁰T			
O		Y		A			I			
N			¹¹M	U	S	I	C			
G			O				K			
¹²F	A	V	O	U	R	I	T	E		
			S				T			

4 Last letter – first letter
1 drum *2* mixture *3* electric *4* concert
5 trumpet *6* trombone *7* enough *8* half
9 fiddle *10* elevator *11* recorder

5 Word search

M	V	I	O	L	I	N	V	R	W
S	G	X	P	I	A	N	O	R	M
R	U	X	Q	K	T	H	V	E	F
B	I	D	L	X	J	V	S	C	L
F	T	R	U	M	P	E	T	O	U
I	A	F	J	O	P	Q	H	R	T
D	R	L	I	D	R	U	M	D	E
D	Q	X	Y	A	H	C	F	E	T
L	Q	S	Q	A	L	O	M	R	N
E	S	A	X	O	P	H	O	N	E

violin – Violine/Geige,
piano – Klavier, **trumpet** – Trompete,
drum – Trommel, **saxophone** – Saxophon
fiddle – Violine/Geige, **guitar** – Gitarre,
recorder – Blockflöte, **flute** – Querflöte

6 Word groups
places in town
department store, hospital, hostel, leisure
centre, police station, restaurant
jobs
engineer, fireman, paramedic,
policewoman, teacher, waiter
clothes
dress, jacket, pyjamas, shoes, skirt, trousers
animals
deer, frog, hedgehog, mole, squirrel,
woodpecker

Unit 1

1 Word friends
do: a good job, a project, nothing
listen: carefully, to music, to the teacher
get: angry, dressed, ready
have: a baby, a cold, enough time
look: after the baby, different, for the money

2 Word ladder
home, **some**, **same**, **save**, **have**, **hate**, **date**,
late, **lane**, **line**, **fine**, **mine**, **mile**, milk

3 Definitions
1 four – **wheels**
2 important – country – **capital**
3 places – photos – **sights**
4 woman – king – **queen**
5 spend – hotel – **hostel**
6 live – lots – **concert**

4 More about ... London Underground
2 because, *3* only, *4* before, *5* and, *6* but,
7 too, *8* when, *9* more, *10* Although

Lösungen

5 Crossword: places in a city

(crossword grid with answers: HOSPITAL, SQUARE, MUSEUM, LOCK, CHURCH, PALACE, LIBRARY, CATHEDRAL, COLUMN)

6 Hidden words
1 plate, 2 air, 3 plane, 4 lane, 5 ear,
6 train, 7 arm, 8 planet, 9 mail, 10 late,
11 learn

7 Word families
1 explain, 2 win, 3 smile, 4 fly, 5 act,
6 laugh, 7 build, 8 describe,
9 rehearse, 10 glue, 11 move, 12 explore

8 Word building
1 **dancing lessons** – Tanzstunden
2 **family tree** – Stammbaum
3 **sports centre** – Sportzentrum
4 **sound file** – Tondatei
5 **football boots** – Fußballschuhe
6 **film star** – Filmstar
7 **doorbell** – Türklingel
8 **classroom** – Klassenraum
9 **homework** – Hausaufgabe
10 **wheelchair** – Rollstuhl,
11 **football** – Fußball
12 **weekend** – Wochenende

9 Odd word out
1 adult, 2 budgie, 3 CD-player,
4 trendy, 5 dish, 6 ball

10 The best word
1 angry, 2 shy, 3 proud, 4 puzzled,
5 scared, 6 nervous

11 Word search

(word search grid)

Straßenbahn – tram, **Bahnhof** – station,
einsteigen – get on, **Flughafen** – airport,
Flugzeug – plane, **Taxi** – taxi,
Fahrplan – timetable, **aussteigen** – get off,
Bus – bus, **Fähre** – ferry,
Bahnsteig – platform, **Flugsteig** – gate,
Zug – train, **umsteigen** – change,
Auto – car

12 Opposites
1 national, 2 spicy, 3 clean, 4 right,
5 loudly, 6 weak, 7 impossible, 8 leave,
9 rich, 10 closed, 11 single, 12 friends

13 Pronunciation
e – already, bread, breakfast, dead, head, meant
iː – clean, beach, cheap, eastbound, leave, tea
ɪə – dear, clear, disappear, ear, idea, near

14 One or two letters?
fiddle, middle, student, hidden, ready, model
afraid, giraffe, traffic, often, difficult, left
another, beginning, dinner, tunnel, enemy,
pencil

15 Hour glasses

	1	F	E	W
2	W	E	L	S	H
3		C	L	E	A	N
4		F	A	C	T	S
		5	A	T	E
			R
		6	B	I	N
7	B	A	C	O	N
8	S	K	I	R	T
9	A	F	T	E	R
		10	E	Y	E

	1	F	U	N
2	M	O	N	E	Y
3		T	O	D	A	Y
4		E	N	E	M	Y
		5	A	R	M
			G
		6	A	R	T
7	S	M	O	K	E
8	F	L	U	T	E
9	S	U	N	N	Y
		10	A	D	D

Das geheime Wort lautet:
Englisch – underground
Deutsch – U-Bahn

16 Picture puzzle
a purse, a dice, a pencil sharpener, a pencil, a helmet, a sandwich, an apple, a fish

Unit 2

1 Word friends
1 eat, 2 wait, 3 catch, 4 read, 5 speak, 6 listen, 7 know, 8 do, 9 become, 10 keep

2 The fourth word
1 vegetable, 2 stupid, 3 bakery, 4 flight, 5 pork, 6 bottom, 7 forget, 8 teach, 9 wives

3 Odd word out
1 farm, 2 farmer, 3 danger, 4 salmon, 5 lorry, 6 station, 7 three, 8 first, 7 wait

4 Scrambled words: school
1 **timetable** – Stundenplan
2 **teacher** – Lehrer
3 **classmate** – Klassenkamerad/in
4 **holidays** – (Schul-)Ferien
5 **board** – Tafel
6 **science** – Naturwissenschaft
7 **classroom** – Klassenraum

5 Word groups
farm animals
chicken, sheep, lamb, horse, cow, turkey
media
mobile, television, radio, sound file, magazine, newspaper
transport
arrival, departure, timetable, Tube, bus stop, station

6 Last letter – first letter
1 timetable, 2 excited, 3 departure, 4 elephant, 5 take, 6 elevator, 7 rock, 8 key, 9 you, 10 until, 11 lonely, 12 yawn

7 Spot the mistakes
1 biger: bigger, ilands: islands,
2 Live: Life, lonly: lonely,
3 have: has, mobil: mobile,
4 write: writes. weak: week,
5 musik: music, webseite: website

8 Making phrases
1 take, 2 send, 3 check, 4 feed, 5 get off, 6 phone

9 Number crossword

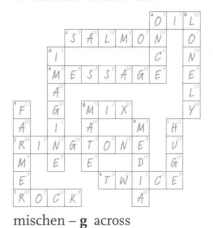

mischen – **g** across
riesig – **i** down
zweimal – **k** across
einsam – **b** down
Medien – **h** down
Kumpel – **g** down
sich (etwas) vorstellen – **d** down
Nachricht – **e** across

10 The best word
1 exciting, 2 strange, 3 sad, 4 huge, 5 realistic

11 Word pairs
catch – ball, **do** – course, **download** – sound file, **pack** – rucksack, **play** – recorder, **read** – menu, **send** – message, **wear** – helmet

12 Words with different meanings
1 **single** – ledig/einfache,
2 **change** – Wechselgeld/umsteigen,
3 **timetable** – Fahrplan/Stundenplan,
4 **correct** – richtig/korrigieren,
5 **work** – arbeiten/funktionieren,
6 **walk** – zu Fuß gehen/Spaziergan

13 Word search: town and country words

H	H	A	R	B	O	U	R	V	P	B	S
I	T	O	W	E	R	F	S	F	A	R	M
L	D	S	Q	U	A	R	E	K	F	N	C
L	Y	E	Z	C	E	Z	A	R	W	P	R
B	M	L	A	A	B	I	S	L	A	N	D
E	O	A	W	N	R	O	A	D	T	Y	G
A	U	K	J	A	I	T	N	Y	G	I	H
C	N	E	F	L	D	U	Z	Y	Y	W	G
H	T	R	H	M	G	F	I	E	L	D	R
C	A	S	T	L	E	H	C	O	A	S	T
O	I	J	S	T	A	T	I	O	N	C	R
D	N	Z	O	D	R	B	A	Y	S	L	K

sea – Meer, **harbour** – Hafen, **tower** – Turm,
square – Platz, **island** – Insel, **road** – Straße,
field – Feld/Sportplatz, **castle** – Schloss,
coast – Küste, **station** – Bahnhof, **bay** – Bucht,
hill – Hügel, **beach** – Strand, **mountain** – Berg,
lake – See, **canal** – Kanal

14 More about ... Orkney
1 islands *2* on, *3* biggest, *4* and, *5* but,
6 under, *7* another, *8* between, *9* takes,
10 for, *11* make, *12* history

15 Lost words
1 unsafe, *2* healthy, *3* untidy,
4 unhealthy, *5* happy, *6* unfriendly,
7 correct, *8* upset, *9* sorry

16 Vocabulary network
SCHOOL
do: a test, a project on Scotland, homework
work: alone, in a small group,
with a partner
listen to: the CD, an explanation, a recording
SPORTS
play: football, hockey, tennis
go: swimming, riding, surfing
do: judo, sport, yoga
HOBBIES AND FREE TIME
play: the drums, the piano, the trumpet
collect: model cars, postcards, stamps
visit: a friend, grandma, museums

Unit 3

1 Words in pictures
a) *1* face, *2* eye, *3* nose, *4* ear, *5* teeth,
   6 hair, *7* mouth, *8* finger, *9* hand
b) *1* pretty/round, *2* blue/bright,
   3 long/small, *4* my left/right,
   5 broken/white, *6* grey/tidy,
   7 a big/loud, *8* clean/strong

2 Hidden words
1 nose, *2* singer, *3* east, *4* sea, *5* stone,
6 train, *7* star, *8* rain, *9* orange, *10* great,
11 art

3 Word families
a) *2* begin, *3* explain, *4* feel, *5* mean, *6* mix,
   7 move, *8* smoke, *9* phone, *10* practise,
   11 bully, *12* invite, *13* teach, *14* translate
b) *1* meaning – explain, *2* invitation – invite,
   3 practise, *4* phone – arrive, *5* translation

4 Word friends
enter: a building, a room, a shop
score: again, three goals, a point
spot: a mistake, a fire, a hair in the soup
support: my school team, the players, the coach
train: at a sports club, hard, twice a week

5 The fourth word
1 twice, *2* all, *3* female, *4* coach,
5 sex, *6* supporter, *7* unlock, *8* age

6 Verb forms
1 do – did – done
2 beat – beat – beaten
3 break – broke – broken
4 begin – began – begun
5 cut – cut – cut
6 fight – fought – fought
7 mean – meant – meant
8 upset – upset – upset

7 Definitions
1 washes – hair: **hairdresser**
2 looks – person: **clone**
3 team – matches: **supporter**
4 last – winner: **final**
5 country – pigs: **farmer**
6 most – school: **head teacher**

8 Word ladder
need – **feed – feet – meet – meat – beat – boat –
boot – book – took – cook – look – lock** – luck

9 Last letter – first letter
1 stress, *2* support, *3* train, *4* news, *5* shirt,
6 travel, *7* lessons, *8* stew, *9* words,
10 ship, *11* papers, *12* stadium, *13* meaning,
14 goalkeeper, *15* realistic

10 Pronunciation
ə – colour, famous, harbour, nervous
aʊ – around, cloud, house, proud
uː – group, soup, through, you
ʌ – cousin, double, enough, touch
ɔː – bought, course, yours, thought

11 Crossword

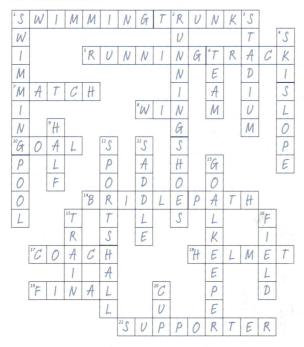

12 More about ... Manchester United

1 club, 2 times, 3 third, 4 over, 5 millions, 6 rich, 7 players, 8 huge, 9 match, 10 even, 11 than, 12 learn

13 Hour glasses

1 SPY, 2 CLOUD, 3 RULER, 4 SHIRT, 5 ICE, 6 TWO, 7 SCORE, 8 ROMAN, 9 TRAIN, 10 END

1 WHO, 2 COACH, 3 PRIZE, 4 HURRY, 5 ADD, 6 PEN, 7 UPSET, 8 ESSAY, 9 STEEL, 10 ART

Das geheime Wort lautet:
Englisch – hairdresser, Deutsch – Friseur/in

14 Odd word out

1 journey, 2 goalkeeper, 3 bat, 4 semi-final, 5 meal, 6 appetite, 7 pitch, 8 hope

15 Word search

room
bed, chair, cupboard, lamp, shelf, sofa, table, wardrobe
clothes
anorak, pullover, shoe, shorts, skirt, sock, trainers, trousers
transport
bus, ferry, lorry, plane, ship, taxi, tram, underground
sport
athletics, court, goal, medal, Paralympics, skis, stadium, volleyball
food
chips, hamburger, pizza, salad, sausage, soup, spaghetti, stew

Unit 4

1 Lost words

1 at, 2 against, 3 on, 4 until, 5 inside, 6 to, 7 about, 8 onto, 9 across, 10 about, 11 in

2 School words

1 board, 2 choir, 3 class, 4 students, 5 history, 6 biology, 7 pencil, 8 teacher, 9 art, 10 essay

Das geheime Wort lautet:
Englisch – dictionary, Deutsch – Wörterbuch

3 Word pairs
build – stadium, **call** – ambulance,
climb – mountain, **cook** – stew,
correct – mistake, **grow** – lettuce,
listen to – live music, **read** – magazine,
score – goal, **turn on** – light,
wear – football shirt, **win** – medal

4 One or two letters?
reggae, begin, language, biggest, fog, foggy
collect, adult, until, talent, model, pullover
community, swimmer, woman, grammar, moment, thermometer
report, shopping, pepper, supporter, represent, disappear
diary, married, guitar, tired, hurry, different
promise, essay, glasses, guess, husband, island
bottle, water, pretty, weather, spaghetti

5 Vocabulary network
TRAVEL
visit: a castle, an old church, a museum
pack: a suitcase, a bag, a rucksack
go: by train, on holiday, on a boat trip
SPORT AND FREE TIME
win: a cup, a medal, a prize
go: canoeing, fishing, snowshoeing
wear: running shoes, a helmet, pads
NOT WELL
feel: terrible, ill, weak
have: a sore throat, a cold, a temperature
phone: an ambulance, a doctor, the hospital

6 Spot the mistakes
1 childs: children, has: have
2 realy: really, off: of
3 allso: also, danger: dangerous
4 usualy: usually, errly: early
5 ran: run, swimers: swimmers
6 interresting: interesting, salmons: salmon
7 stand: stands, quitely: quietly
8 bare: bear, jump: jumps

7 Word search

8 Pronunciation
k: knee, know
n: autumn, column
l: folk music, salmon
b: climb, lamb
w: answer, whole
c: scene, science

9 Words with different meanings
1 **square** – Platz/Quadrat-,
2 **colour** – ausmalen/Farbe,
3 **train** – Zug/trainieren,
4 **date** – Datum/Verabredung,
5 **once** – einmal/einst,
6 **final** – Endspiel/letzte,
7 **argument** – Streit/Begründung

10 Odd word out
1 minute, 2 lyrics, 3 per cent, 4 text message,
5 build, 6 sledges, 7 gig, 8 coast

11 The fourth word
1 kilometre, 2 player, 3 themselves,
4 number, 5 instrument, 6 year, 7 moon,
8 knives

12 More about …traditional Inuit hunting
1 temperatures, 2 much, 3 fishing, 4 land,
5 just, 6 kind, 7 used, 8 could, 9 built,
10 about

13 Number crossword

Provinz – **e** across, Mikrophon – **o** across,
beliebt – **g** down, streng – **i** down,
Erwachsene(r) – **n** across, Streit – **l** across,
Messer – **f** down, ärgern – **m** across

14 Word groups
jobs:
actor, cleaner, farmer, painter, shop assistant, waiter
music:
choir, chorus, lyrics, instrument, concert, song
station:
suitcases, toilets, timetable, ticket machines, railway, platforms, trains
weather:
cloudy, fog, rain, snow, stormy, sunny, tornado

15 Opposites
1 strict, 2 disagree, 3 modern, 4 off,
5 under, 6 leave, 7 bottom, 8 remember,
9 departures, 10 wife, 11 boring, 12 cold,
13 dirty, 14 upstairs

Unit 5

1 Pronunciation
ʊ – bully, full, pull, put, push, sugar
juː – computer, community, excuse, huge, menu, tube
ʌ – but, fun, publish, summer, tunnel, trumpet

2 Last letter – first letter
1 chorus, 2 success, 3 successful, 4 leader,
5 rapids, 6 spelling, 7 grandma, 8 announce,
9 editor, 10 revise, 11 electric, 12 curry,
13 yes, 14 section

3 Word families
1 announce, 2 revise, 3 spell, 4 draw, 5 end,
6 live, 7 attack, 8 support,
9 record, 10 laugh

4 Making phrases
1 turn, 2 warn, 3 believe, 4 disagree,
5 grow, 6 look, 7 escape

5 The fourth word
1 vegetable, 2 dish, 3 bird, 4 month,
5 instrument, 6 planet, 7 colour, 8 art

6 Definitions
1 ears – radio: headphones
2 work – more: strike
3 spend – home: sleepover
4 corrects – texts: editor
5 picture – pen: drawing
6 everybody – noise: silence

7 Hour glasses

1	A	D	D	
2	Q	U	E	E	N
3	U	P	S	E	T
4	F	A	C	T	S
5		T	R	Y	
		I		
6	S	P	Y	
7	U	N	T	I	L
8	Q	U	I	E	T
9	P	R	O	O	F
10	E	N	D	

1	A	T	E	
2	D	I	R	T	Y
3	B	E	A	C	H
4	M	E	D	A	L
5	K	I	D	
		T		
6	B	I	N	
7	C	H	O	I	R
8	F	I	N	A	L
9	S	T	A	G	E
10	I	L	L	

Das geheime Wort lautet:
Englisch – traditional, Deutsch traditionell

8 Word ladder
film – **file** – **fine** – **line** – **mine** – **mile** – **male** –
mole – **hole** – **role** – **rule** – **rude** – **ride** – **hide** –
side – size

9 Word building
1 bold print: Fettdruck
2 car park: Parkplatz
3 chat room: Chatroom
4 running shoes: Laufschuhe, Sportschuhe
5 text message: SMS
6 semi-final: Halbfinale
7 great-grandfather: Urgroßvater

8 Lösungen

  8 classroom: Klassenzimmer, Klassenraum
  9 snowshoes: Schneeschuhe
10 wheelchair: Rollstuhl

10 Odd word out
1 racket, *2* stadium, *3* score, *4* skate,
5 pipe, *6* silence, *7* monitor, *8* puzzle

11 Words in pictures: fruit and vegetables
  1 bright, red, tomatoes
  2 delicious, forest, mushrooms
  3 sweet, Spanish, oranges
  4 hard, green, apples
  5 big, garden, onions
  6 delicious, German, strawberries
  7 bright, orange, carrots
  8 healthy, green, lettuce
  9 delicious, new, potatoes
10 long, yellow, bananas

12 Opposites
1 worst, *2* bad, *3* top, *4* dark, *5* unhealthy,
6 old-fashioned, *7* late, *8* untidy, *9* behind,
10 answer, *11* noise, *12* arrival, *13* right,
14 forget

13 The best word
1 final, *2* strict, *3* artificial, *4* silly, *5* relaxed,
6 useful, *7* scared

14 Hidden words
1 cinema, *2* listen, *3* tram, *4* castle *5* scan,
6 tunnel, *7* uncle, *8* mice, *9* sister,
10 summer/autumn, *11* clean

15 Word search – The media

E	Z	M	O	N	I	T	O	R	H	P	C
D	M	A	G	A	Z	I	N	E	E	U	Q
I	K	Z	W	B	H	X	N	N	A	B	T
T	O	J	E	O	P	R	A	E	D	L	M
O	R	E	C	O	R	D	R	W	P	I	O
R	H	V	D	K	O	R	T	S	H	S	B
Y	E	L	Z	S	G	E	I	P	O	H	I
G	F	R	T	U	R	P	C	A	N	X	L
R	A	D	I	O	A	O	L	P	E	B	E
N	Z	D	G	K	M	R	E	E	S	G	H
W	N	E	W	S	M	T	Q	R	D	V	W
S	U	T	E	L	E	V	I	S	I	O	N

monitor – Bildschirm
magazine – Zeitschrift
record – aufnehmen/Schallplatte
radio – Radio
news – Nachrichten
television – Fernsehen
editor – Redakteur/in
book – Buch
programme – Programm
report – Bericht
article – Artikel
newspaper – Zeitung
headphones – Kopfhörer
publish – veröffentlichen
mobile – Handy/Mobiltelefon

16 Word friends
1 revise, *2* produce, *3* make, *4* record, *5* play,
6 go, *7* be, *8* have, *9* laugh, *10* skim,
11 keep, *12* remember

17 Scrambled words: American and British English
1 movie, film *2* mom, mum *3* elevator, lift
4 subway, underground *5* vacation, holidays

18 Crossword